Ready?
Get Set . . .
It's LifeTime!

Please forward any questions, comments or requests to:

It's LifeTime!
P.O. Box 6473
Silver Spring, MD 20906
www.itslifetime.com
info@itslifetime.com

This book is written as a source of entertainment and information only. The suggestions made are not to substitute qualified, professional help.

First Edition

Gooding, Frederick & Sharon.
Ready? Get Set . . . It's LifeTime!/Frederick & Sharon Gooding.-1st ed.

ISBN 978-0-9778048-2-5

Published by On the Reelz Press

Printed in the United States of America

Jacta Alea Est

Zachary,

DEDICATION

"

For those committed
to a lifetime of success!"

I applaud you and
I hope that you will
make a legacy for
this family. Perserverance
is the key to success.
when you fall down
you brush yourself
off and continue to
move forward.

Love you
Aunt Penny
2012

P.S. Please read!

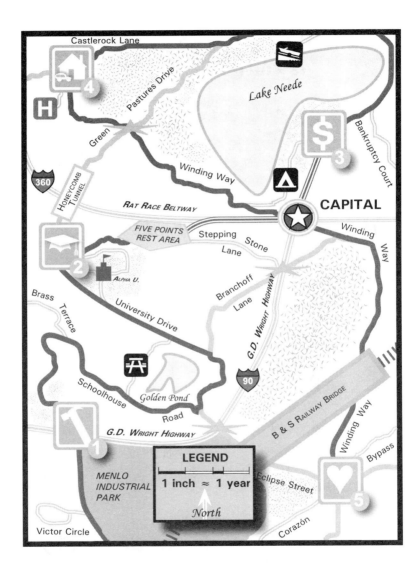

Castlerock Lane

Lake Neede

Pastures Drive

Green

Winding Way

360

Honeycomb Tunnel

Rat Race Beltway

Bankruptcy Court

CAPITAL

Winding Way

Five Points Rest Area

Stepping Stone Lane

Brass Terrace

Alpha U.

University Drive

Branchoff Lane

G.D. Wright Highway

90

Schoolhouse

Golden Pond

Road

B & S Railway Bridge

Winding Way

Bypass

G.D. Wright Highway

Eclipse Street

LEGEND

1 inch ≈ 1 year

North

Menlo Industrial Park

Corazón

Victor Circle

TABLE OF CONTENTS

CHAPTER ZERO:
READY? GET SET . . .

WHO are you? WHO do you want to be? WHO do you want to meet? WHO will you work with? WHO will you love? WHO will respect you? WHO will pay you for your time? **WHAT** do you want to do? WHAT will it cost you? WHAT must you sacrifice? WHAT can you do? WHAT is it worth? WHAT will keep you stimulated? WHAT will keep you satisfied? **WHEN** will you start? WHEN will you will be ready? WHEN will you stop? t you made it? WHEN will yo will you start? **WHERE** can d? WHERE do you want to can you find reliable help? o you want to live? **WHY** succee try? WHY chase after your dreams? WHY believe? WHY is it worth it? WHY do you want it? WHY are you unsure? WHY do you think you know the answer? **HOW** will you succeed? HOW will you execute your plan? HOW will you get started? HOW will you know when it is time to change? HOW will you find reliable help? HOW will you know that you have arrived? HOW can you chart

CHAPTER ZERO
START YOUR ENGINE

Are you ready for **Life**? We hope so! Well, ready or not, life is ready for you! In fact, it has been waiting patiently for quite some time now . . . .

Do you hear that? **The clock is ticking!** *For who and for what you ask?* Why, the clock and its alarm bells chime for thee! Quite simply, the time has come to figure out the rest of your life. No pressure, right? Well, even if you do feel pressure, there is no need for alarm – just a plan instead.

A *planned* course of action is strongly recommended in order to maximize your chances for success in this **LifeTime**. Why? The more concrete your plan, the more likely you will create for yourself solid opportunities to succeed. While the mere creation of a plan does not guarantee success, it is infinitely more difficult to obtain success without one. Now then, where or how do you begin? Why, at the beginning! Yet, this chapter is entitled "Chapter Zero" because it is an obvious, but overlooked starting point.

Typically when counting, people start with the number one and skip the number zero. Similarly, when it comes to success, many start by talking about their desired results while skipping over the fundamental steps necessary to achieve such results. Thus, before we begin in earnest, we take the time to properly introduce key concepts developed throughout the book. This way, there will be "zero" chance of confusion! That being said, let's get this show on the road!

READY?

This manuscript is for the Young Adult who wants to "make it," "have it all," or generally "be successful" in life, but is not 100% clear about *how* that success is actually going to occur. We thereby provide practical pointers about "this thing called life" so that you do not spend most of your time earning success the hard way. After all, why make the same mistakes that we made early in life when you do not have to?

Alas, we cannot prevent all Young Adults from making mistakes, since mistakes are a natural part of life. Yet, we can help you prepare for the road ahead by minimizing common detours caused by *manageable* and *preventable* mistakes. This proactive approach will enable you to travel through life more comfortably positioned in the "driver's seat." So then, do you have the drive to succeed? If you do, then keep the pages (and wheel) turning.

F.Y.EYE

As you navigate your way through the following pages, keep a sharp eye out for the following *Road Signs for Success*:

ROAD SIGNS for SUCCESS

No Bones about It
Practical anecdotes about the road ahead

Watch for Bull
Friendly alerts to unfriendly distractions

Real-Road Crossing
Signals the intersection of two or more *Decision Points*

Connect the Dots
"Road games" to drive key points home

No Magic Here
Mini-reviews posted throughout the text

Cheesy but True
Obvious, but insightful insights

ROADMAP to SUCCESS

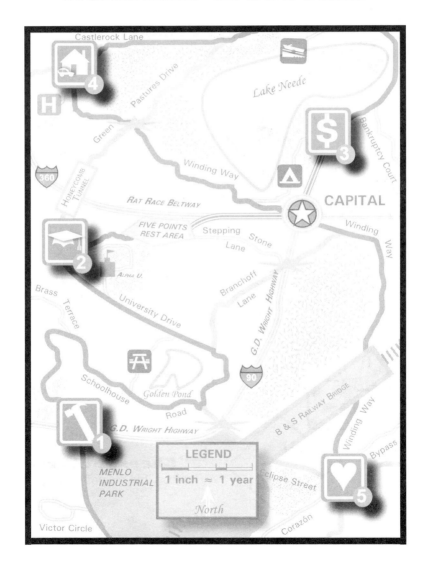

GET SET . . .

To prepare you for the road ahead, we have identified five major aspects of adult life that you will likely navigate during your journey to success in your **LifeTime**. Accordingly, the book is structured around the following five **Decision Points**:

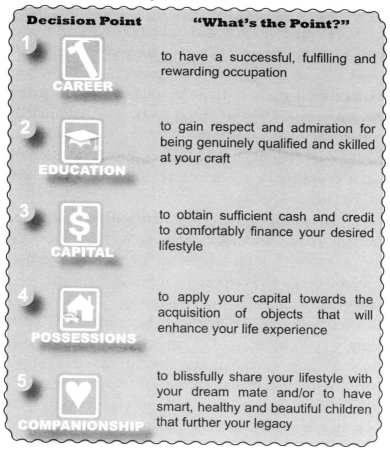

Decision Point	"What's the Point?"
1 CAREER	to have a successful, fulfilling and rewarding occupation
2 EDUCATION	to gain respect and admiration for being genuinely qualified and skilled at your craft
3 CAPITAL	to obtain sufficient cash and credit to comfortably finance your desired lifestyle
4 POSSESSIONS	to apply your capital towards the acquisition of objects that will enhance your life experience
5 COMPANIONSHIP	to blissfully share your lifestyle with your dream mate and/or to have smart, healthy and beautiful children that further your legacy

>> **NOTE** <<
The Decision Points *are presented in a specific sequence meant to maximize your chances for success. Using our experiences as a guide, we believe our order is the most effective approach, although you are certainly free to change the order and structure your own path.*

Now, everyone wants "to be successful," right? But what exactly does that mean? Success is such a vague term that without any context, it makes statements such as "I want to be successful," or "I want a successful life" almost useless to us. Therefore, **success** will be our little code word for **your happiness**. Only you and you alone will ultimately determine the true meaning of "success." Yet, to assist with your definition, we offer practical pointers on what to anticipate when you reach any or all of life's major *Decision Points*.

Despite the general popularity of our designated *Decision Points*, understandably not *everyone's* concept of "a successful life" consists of getting married, spending their lives chasing a zillion dollars, driving a fancy car, having kids, owning a home, going to college or even working for a living! No problemo. There simply is no hard and fast rule about *what* you must do to be successful – success is relative and is largely based upon individual perception. Nonetheless, it is important to clearly identify as early as possible what exactly will meet *your* definition of success.

Further, by crafting your specific definition of success, you hopefully will become emboldened to stake out your own path and avoid the ever-crowded **Rat Race**. The *Rat Race* refers to the daily struggle to survive and get ahead in an increasingly competitive and capitalistic society (i.e., the "daily grind").

So, if a winding, circuitous route extending towards the sunset represents the long road to success, then a large circular race track wherein participants race endlessly around in circles represents the *Rat Race*. Hence, forward progress is exceedingly ambiguous within the *Rat Race* since competitors only take occasional, time-pressured pit stops just to gear up for even more racing around and around the track.

In the *Rat Race*, competitors hardly ever experience true progress because they are stuck in the vicious cycle that we refer to as the "daily grind."

Essentially, the daily grind refers to all the things you dislike doing on a daily basis, but *have to do* in order to survive from day to day.

Since maintaining your position within the *Rat Race* is so time-consuming, typically it is very difficult to suddenly "switch gears" once you have already started upon a career track. Instead, you may find yourself speeding around the *Rat Race* track in attempts to improve your position, but feel that you are getting nowhere fast. Plus, *Rat Race* victories are notoriously short-lived since there is no obvious end point in sight on a circular and repetitive track!

In contrast to the *Rat Race*, the **Road to Success** is a long, winding and unpredictable road indeed. The *Road to Success* road is unpredictable in that its exact pathway varies widely depending upon one's own definition of success (and belief on where it is "located"). The *Road to Success* is also random since there is no consistent "fast track" to success despite late-night infomercials and junk e-mails to the contrary.

We admit: the *Road to Success* is often fraught with delays, detours, obstacles, accidents and inclement weather. Yet, the *Road to Success* can simultaneously surprise you with interesting fellow travelers, timely shortcuts, breathtaking views and picturesque panoramas – all of which help to make your trip worthwhile. The key is knowing where you want your *Road to Success* to take you – *ahead of time*.

To ensure that you find your desired happiness, now is as good a time as any to sit down and get set with a plan or roadmap. Otherwise, you run the risk of getting stuck in gridlocked *Rat Race* traffic or losing your way along the *Road to Success*.

LET'S GO!

If you have ever been on a lengthy road trip, then you know that any standard trip involves a bit of pre-planning. The "spontaneous" method of just getting up and leaving without consulting a map or ever looking at the gas gauge always seems to work in the movies, but it is never quite the same in **real life**. Simple decisions ranging from what music to pack, to double-checking tire pressure, to selecting the best highway routes are all made at the very important preparatory and planning stages.

Of course, any plan, no matter how well designed, will demand from you the flexibility to adapt and respond as the circumstances require. After all, one cannot possibly plan for *every* conceivable event or contingency. Regardless, **a revised plan beats a non-existent plan any day of the week**.

Most people who plan to be successful, plan out their actions ahead of time. Here are a few examples:

>> *any coach of any team will tell you the same; the team reviews a game plan that it must execute before going out to "play ball"*

>> *any corporate employee will tell you the same; they have meetings upon meetings upon meetings to plan future actions for the good of the company*

>> *any professor worth her salt will tell you the same; she hands out lesson plans and syllabi the first few days of class that span weeks and months into the future*

Most "successful" people plan ahead and map out their future actions in order to maximize the best results. Equally as important, successful people revisit and revise their plans where appropriate and necessary. Quite simply, the more you prepare now, the more confident you will feel about upcoming decisions that will unmistakably affect your future success.

The purpose of this book is not to alarm you, but rather to alert you to *manageable* and *preventable* mistakes that all too often become detours and roadblocks for ambitious Young Adults. This means that rather than provide a *practical guarantee* to success, **It's LifeTime!** serves as a *practical guide* for major life-decisions that impact your ability to achieve the success you desire. Please, gain foresight from our hindsight.

But wait a minute – do you hear that? *The clock is ticking!* It's time to get going! In other words:

It's LifeTime!

SUCCESSFULLY YOURS
- Frederick & Sharon Gooding
2007

CHAPTER 1:
CAREER

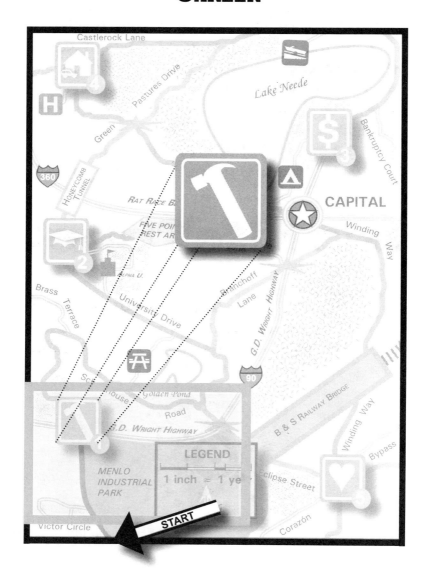

13

THE ROAD AHEAD

Work in Progress

Working Double-Time

CEO of YOU, Inc.

Job vs. Career

But, What to Do?

An Innocent Enough
Question

START

The first stop on our journey is **Career**. At this *Decision Point*, we explore strategies to help you identify your future occupation as accurately as possible.

At **An Innocent Enough Question** we help you develop a response to the frequently lobbed query "What do you want to do when you grow up?"

We then help you explore potential work options in **But, What to Do?**

Although we encourage working wherever and whenever you can, at **Jobs vs. Career** we fine tune the difference between finding a job and creating a career; one is merely existing, the other is truly living.

Next, at **CEO of YOU, Inc.** we further reinforce the idea of knowing your interests and understanding your worth while out in the open job market.

Then, in **Working Double-Time** we insist that you "think twice" when *planning ahead*; you may change your mind about what you ultimately want to do.

Lastly, at **Work in Progress** we encourage you to evaluate every working opportunity – but with roadmap in mind.

CHAPTER ONE
Charting a Course

COURSE PREVIEW

Our first stop is **Career**. In mapping out your life, plan to center most of your future actions around that which you intend to do on a daily basis. Sure, not everyone can identify *exactly* what they want to do when the future is so far away. Still, by planning ahead, you can bring the future within reach. Why? *Thinking concretely about your employment scenario helps make your employment scenario more concrete.*

We start with **Career** because decisions you make concerning your future aspirations will significantly shape the course of your entire **LifeTime**. Period. When people think of their future career prospects, they usually think about the ability to make money – and hopefully lots of it! Yet, as ironic as it sounds, a "simple" decision that may only take you seconds to make today, will affect most of your future actions for years to come.

Whether you wish to work within the public or private sector, it is unavoidable – you earn a living by doing *something* for other people. Whether you decide to make a living by pedaling a product or by providing a service, you do not just randomly start selling to the market. *If you plan to work, you need to work up a plan.*

AN INNOCENT ENOUGH QUESTION

*"So, what do you want to do
when you grow up?"*

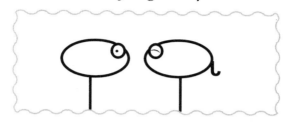

Ah, the dreaded question. We are sure that by now, you have heard some variation of the above question since "grow up" can be replaced with a number of common words and phrases such as "graduate," "get older," "get done" or even "get out!" If this question causes for your demeanor to darken or sour at social functions whenever your parents' friends or your older relatives beckon you near, then fear not evermore. To alleviate the pressure, all you have to do is politely query in response:

*"Did you know what you wanted to do
when you were my age?"*

If the answer is **no**, then perhaps you exposed your inquisitor as merely encouraging you to think about this topic early on in life. Do not feel angst or worry. There is still time enough for you to figure out: 1) what your goals are and 2) how you intend to accomplish them. Take note that many a successful adult did not have complete clarity about their future career when he or she was your age.

Now, if your inquisitor answers you with a **yes**, then you still win. For what you do next is take a knee and listen patiently to their story. Understanding how a person locks into their passion or purpose is useful in recognizing the same process when it happens to you – especially if you are unsure about your life's eventual path to begin with.

No Magic Here:

Typically, you must acquire some type of education before you pursue your career. Therefore, thinking about your career **first** will help you determine what type of education and/or training that you (and your career) will need.

BUT WHAT TO DO?

Selecting an occupation requires that you envision a role that you will assume in society. When it comes to figuring out how to define that role, why reinvent the wheel? Why not build upon the momentum amassed from generations before you? If fortunate enough to inherit the goodwill of a family business, then you possibly may enjoy the financial security that usually accompanies an established business as opposed to "starting from scratch." Or, are your folks doing something that interests you? If so, do your parents possess craft or trade skills that you can apprentice and market for yourself?

Now, if you are not smitten with the idea of following in your mother or father's footsteps, then it is time to make your own tracks. According to the "go-with-what-you-know" theory, what follows are some suggestions for potential sources of inspiration to help you create a meaningful career path:

>> **Hobbies**
>> **Part-time jobs**
>> **Extra-curricular activities**
>> **Role models**
>> **Tasks that you enjoy**
>> **Daydreams**
>> **"Cool" television or movie roles**
>> **Favorite book characters**
>> **Favorite consumer goods**
>> **"Cool" television commercials**
>> **"Cool" magazine advertisements**
>> **Tasks in which you excel**
>> **Local attractions/museums**

Another way to get yourself started is to think about a topic in which you would like to become an expert. As smart as we all are, at some point in time, we all need help in some form from an expert. Why? *Time is limited.* Conceivably, *we all can learn* how to repair our own cars, file our own taxes, install our own hardwood floors, build our own websites and design and sew our own clothes.

Yet, *we all do not* because not everyone has the time, interest, nor energy to specialize in every conceivable trade or service. Independence aside, you simply cannot "do it yourself" all the time. Instead, you will pay others to perform these desired tasks "for a fee." In turn, once you select and truly master a craft, people will gladly pay you for your "expertise."

Cheesy but True:

Everybody has to work for a living. The trick is to get paid a whole lot of money for doing something that you like a whole lot – and would still want to do even if no one paid you.

The key is to think about a task that you can perform better than the average person (i.e., become an expert), and confidently charge people for the privilege of saving them either time, money or both. To help you brainstorm, what follows on page 20 is a **LIST OF 100** potentially rewarding career tracks that you may or may not have considered. Practically speaking, not everyone can land a high-profile and lucrative career as a professional athlete or an A-list entertainer. In addition to above-average talent, plenty of random *luck* is often required with securing such high-profile and glamorous positions.

Thus, the career options in the **LIST OF 100** underscore multiple ways whereby proper training, pure passion and good old fashioned elbow grease will help you capitalize upon your untapped potential. Now, as with all good things, *you will also need a bit o' luck* along the way since chance is usually a standard part of any formula for success. Still, if armed with a sound roadmap, you will need considerably *less luck* than what is required to become a professional athlete or an A-list entertainer.

Now, of course there are more than just these 100 possible career options available to you. Thus, the **LIST OF 100** also serves as a healthy reminder that there are a myriad of career options "out there" for you to explore outside of the highly celebrated doctor/lawyer or entertainer/athlete paradigms. Quite simply, there are many different ways to secure for yourself a financially comfortable lifestyle. So now is as good a time as any to start exploring and determine which options suit you best. The **LIST OF 100** is as follows:

LIST OF 100

1) meteorologist 2) air traffic controller 3) court reporter 4) landscaper 5) climatologist 6) park ranger 7) paralegal 8) nurse 9) cable television installer 10) librarian 11) architect 12) website designer 13) journalist 14) pilot (commercial or private) 15) meteorologist 16) school teacher 17) automotive mechanic 18) car salesman 19) oil rigger 20) police officer 21) university professor 22) real estate agent 23) firefighter 24) copy editor 25) graphic designer 26) fast food franchisee 27) painter 28) carpenter 29) wedding planner 30) plumber 31) construction contractor 32) studio engineer 33) home inspector 34) taxi/limousine driver 35) occupational therapist 36) speech pathologist 37) mortgage broker 38) park ranger 39) mechanical engineer 40) stock trader 41) personal trainer 42) postal worker 43) IT specialist (information technology) 44) insurance broker 45) biologist 46) physician's assistant 47) tailor/seamstress 48) forestry technician 49) geologist 50) optometrist 51) pharmacist 52) psychologist 53) urban planner 54) social worker 55) accountant 56) archeologist 57) special educator 58) private investigator 59) electrical engineer 60) consultant 61) photographer 62) make up artist 63) anthropologist 64) computer repair technician 65) mediator/dispute resolution specialist 66) copy writer 67) locomotive engineer 68) fisherman 69) oceanographer 70) sound technician 71) caterer 72) banker 73) restaurant chef 74) language translator 75) security specialist 76) metallurgist 77) appraiser 78) statistician 79) botanist 80) television/movie camera operator 81) water technician 82) hotel manager 83) import/export broker 84) clinical researcher 85) chemist 86) welder 87) television news anchor 88) aviation mechanic 89) travel agent 90) massage therapist 91) switchboard operator 92) event planner 93) disc jockey 94) public relations specialist 95) museum curator 96) crane operator 97) tour guide 98) beautician 99) barber/hair stylist 100) civil engineer

JOB vs. CAREER

Job versus career. We cannot stress enough how important it is to think about these two concepts early and often. For the difference between *"finding a job"* and *"creating your career"* is the difference between existing and living.

Finding a job refers to finding *any* job – literally *anything* – that provides you with a paycheck. Essentially, it means finding employment that meets your short-term financial needs but may not necessarily satisfy your long-term professional goals. As a result, you may not stay long at this job due to the absence of a deep, personal connection to your work.

Examples of *Finding a Job*:

>> *video store clerk*
>> *summer camp counselor*
>> *bookstore sales associate*
>> *grocery stocker*

Creating your career is more about feeling empowered by something that you enjoy and find stimulating, as well as financially rewarding. Also, when creating your career, you remain in the driver's seat and have more control over your future direction. What follows are examples of how the four jobs listed above can blossom into well-paying careers.

Examples of *Creating Your Career*:

>> *movie studio executive*
>> *director of after-school programs*
>> *author*
>> *gourmet food distributor*

Now bear in mind these two general rules: 1) everybody works for somebody (even if this means "working for yourself") and 2) everyone makes a living selling *something* (i.e., a product or a service). Thus, based upon the personal goals you wish to reach, which option offers you the best chance to reach your goals: a **job** or a **career**?

Bear in mind that a **job** typically refers to a short-term solution for your immediate financial needs. While it is possible to find a job doing something you like replete with great perks and good pay, the bottom line is that you are still working for someone else. **With a job, you sell your time to the market**. Therefore, someone else directly profits from your expertise and labor. Also, in securing a job, your creative independence may be compromised since you work at the direct behest of someone else and for the overall benefit of your employer.

That being said, you can still maintain some power over your ultimate destiny by ensuring that the job position you choose aligns with your long-term professional goals. Thus, if within your heart-of-hearts you wish to become an architect, you may want to re-think that summer job at the mall. Although working summer jobs at the mall will not automatically prevent you from becoming an architect, you must question yourself practically about how the money, energy and time you spend working your summer job will advance you towards your end goals and ultimate vision.

A **career** represents a long-term occupational commitment within a defined industry or trade and is typically more open-ended with respect to career trajectory and compensation. Many careers also require specialized training before you are allowed to hold yourself out to the marketplace as an expert. **With a career, you sell your knowledge to the market**.

No Bones about It:

Everybody makes a living selling something, whether it be a product or a service. What will you sell and how will you personally profit?

So, why the distinction? From the get-go, we want to encourage you to think creatively about your career. In short, do not just settle for a "dead end" job and assume a *Rat Race* lifestyle and mentality. We are not "anti-job," we are anti-*bad*-job. Essentially, whenever or however possible, we encourage you to control the means of your own production. Thus, if you carefully sift through your job options with a defined career choice in mind, you may also increase your eventual chances of obtaining the independence, flexibility and financial success that you desire. The key is figuring out how to leverage your job experiences so that they can propel you further into your career plans.

No Magic Here:

Job = *existing*; fulfills short-term financial needs as you sell your time to the market
Career = *living*; fulfills long-term personal goals as you sell your knowledge to the market

The more informed you are, the more adept you become about making decisions concerning your career trajectory. Interestingly enough, you will soon discover that **pay, while certainly important, is not the most important criteria in selecting a position**. Rather, a good indication that you are in the "right place," is if your work satisfies both components of *competency* and *compatibility*.

For *competency*, you should feel confident in what you are doing as you build yourself up as a master of your craft (see "Pipe Dreams," page 45). With *compatibility*, you should feel connected to your work environment. For instance, if you know what you are doing, but feel you are not supported or appreciated (i.e., competency, but not compatibility), your work production will likely decrease over time.

However, if you are a master of your craft and not only feel supported, but excel when constructively challenged by your peers (i.e., competency plus compatibility), then you are likely headed for long-term success in your profession. Getting a feel for your career plan beforehand will help you run a lesser risk of being "held hostage" by either your paycheck or the *Rat Race* once you do start working.

WORKING DOUBLE-TIME

We just spoke about choosing a career over a job. Now, the next strategy we heavily endorse is the deliberate planning for at least *two* careers. Why? Well, times change and so do people – and so might your career goals. Here is what we mean by two careers:

Career #1 = *training-based; receive tutelage and direction in exchange for a FIXED salary or wages*

Career #2 = *entrepreneurial-based; apply prior training within the free market in exchange for an OPEN-ENDED income*

Your *first career* should focus on obtaining practical experience and training about the industry you are interested in exploring. This includes your prior *jobs*, or the experiences leading up to your current position. While these early job positions may have been of average/below-average pay, such experiences will only increase in value if placed within a larger pattern of opportunities that help you obtain a deeper and richer understanding of your industry or trade.

However, your *second career* should focus on harnessing the training and tutelage gained from your first career and channeling it into an entrepreneurial venture. In other words, the information that you acquire from your first career can be utilized as the foundation for your second career. Additionally, in your second career, look to build upon your professional expertise amassed so far and profit even further from the direct sale of your knowledge to the open marketplace. Consider the following examples:

Career #1	**Career #2**
1. *Chef*	*Restaurateur*
2. *Lawyer*	*Mediator*
3. *Electrician*	*General Contractor*
4. *Music Teacher*	*Music Store Owner*
5. *Investment Banker*	*Venture Capitalist*

Notice how the positions listed in the first column are in fact *careers*. Whether you are working for yourself or with someone else, the positions in column one represent livelihoods whereby you sell your knowledge to the marketplace. Meanwhile, the second column combines both your knowledge *and experience*. Having two career options in mind with overlapping skills ensures that your initial experience and education will not fall to the wayside, should you opt to change careers. Don't you just love those movie scenes when our hero, after having a "light bulb moment," tells their boss to **"shove it"?** After realizing what truly makes them happy, they then boldly begin pursuing their true passion instead of suffering through the pressures of the "daily grind."

Well, let's pretend that your life is not a movie and that for whatever reason, the "happily ever after" scene may not be as easily acted out in *your* life script. Let's also pretend that if you *did* tell your boss off, that you would not have six months of living expenses stored under your mattress at the ready, and that you would worry about "details" such as: *Who am I going to put on my résumé as a reference from my last job? How long will it take me to land my next job? Will my next job pay less than my former job?*

So, if you decide to "alter your course" for whatever reason, it is more preferable to build upon the experiences that you have already acquired as opposed to starting over again from scratch. You should also plan for the market to change and plan to be flexible enough to adapt to those changes as well. Because of the *Rat Race* and its "daily grind" described earlier in *Chapter Zero: Ready? Get Set . . .* , many adults who want to change career tracks simply cannot. Instead, they end up feeling stuck doing what they *have to do* rather than doing what they *want to do*.

No Magic Here:

Career #1 = *training-based*; fixed salary or wages

Career #2 = *entrepreneurial-based*; open-ended income

By planning for two careers *ahead of time*, you will be better equipped to avoid "dead ends" and continue your journey towards your vocational goals. Not only do we stress the selection of a career over a job, but with a **two-career plan** in place, you will also feel doubly prepared (and not perplexed) about what direction to take in the road ahead.

CEO OF YOU, INC.

Whether your salary range is set before you even apply for a position, or whether you personally set the rates that you end up charging clients, you are still the **CEO of YOU, Inc**. In other words, you need to see yourself as Chief Executive Officer (or CEO) of a private enterprise that either sells your labor directly to the open market, or "contracts" out your labor to an employer (i.e., you agree to sell your time to a third party in exchange for wages). In either case, the major challenge that awaits you is *knowing your interests* and *understanding your worth*.

As president and CEO of YOU, Inc., you must adopt a take-control mindset at all times because it fosters the type of confidence required for success in your **LifeTime**. Typically, when searching for employment, you will naturally attempt to meet standards and criteria as set forth by your potential employer. Truth be told, unless you possess a rare skill or some highly-coveted talent that people simply cannot wait to pay you for, your prospective employer will have more leverage than you. Why? Simply because your employer has the job (**$**) that you seek.

Yet, even though you may not have most of the leverage in such an exchange, do recall that you nonetheless have something valuable to offer! Protect *your* value by negotiating or questioning key terms at the beginning of the relationship, rather than merely accept everything presented to you. In fact, when applying for positions, rather than feel completely at your interviewer's mercy, we encourage you to bring to your interview a short, pre-prepared list of open-ended questions that you can pose to your potential colleagues. Why? Quite simply, to eliminate guesswork about your expected performance. You will also gain some extra interview "points" just for being more prepared than the average applicant.

Now, sometimes, you *have to* take a job offer without asking any questions just because you need the money. Nevertheless, if you take a position that you do not particularly care for, be very clear about what you are doing, why you are doing it, and for how long you plan to do it. Think creatively about how your job experience will serve as "training" for your eventual career choice(s).

Otherwise, if you take a job with *pay* and not with a long-term *payoff* in mind, you run the risk of becoming a very compromised member of the *Rat Race*. Quite simply, in "chasing the cheese" (i.e., blindly pursuing **cash money** just for the sake of it), you may make yourself vulnerable to manipulation by those who have the "cheese" that you are chasing.

Conversely, the CEO of YOU, Inc. mindset naturally facilitates self-sufficiency through entrepreneurship. Entrepreneurship requires critical thinking skills, business savvy and social finesse to convert your expertise into a tangible source of capital. The successful application of these skills fosters a heightened degree of self-autonomy and independence. Hence, the CEO of YOU, Inc. mindset dictates that you see yourself as working **with** your employer (including you) towards relevant business goals. This mindset contrasts with the less proactive mindset of working **for** your employer's sole benefit, which is more typical of the "daily grind" outlook.

Watch for Bull:

CAUTION: Do not chase jobs with *high pay*, but rather career positions with *high payoffs*.

While we suggest that working for yourself will eventually afford you the maximum degree of personal freedom and autonomy, let's also add, that starting your own business does not guarantee your own success in any way shape or form. Nor does it mean that you will never have to work for anyone else again in life. Ironically, working for yourself often requires for you to work "harder" and invest proportionally more money, energy and time due to the additional responsibilities that you agree to bear.

While entrepreneurship might not be for everyone, you can still maintain a CEO of YOU, Inc. mindset so that your presence and ability command respect and admiration wherever you work. Remember though, *your* definition of a successful career will serve as your guide. In fact, your personal status as CEO of YOU, Inc. will also be the driving force behind the success of your business affairs. For instance, have you ever heard the phrase **"it's just business, not personal"**? This phrase is probably the most misleading statement we have ever heard, for if business is not personal, then what is it?

Think about it this way: are we robots? No! We are people, and people are personal. Further, people personally profit from the growth of interpersonal relationships or "networking." So, when people conduct business, it is for personal reasons. Lest we forget, when people make business decisions, these decisions affect other people. Period. When you next hear, "it's just business, not personal," just be sure to look for a red flag waving behind that person's head. The reason being, if the decision is not in someway personal, that what else could it be?

As CEO of YOU, Inc., it is generally good practice to take your business "personally" and see to it that your decisions are calculated to delivering the very best work product that you can muster at all times. If you build a better mousetrap, the world will beat a path to your door. No need to chase the cheese!

WORK IN PROGRESS

What follows are some practical pointers to bear in mind as you endeavor to determine whether a job or career best suits your interests:

Research

Quite simply, **there is no perfect profession**. However, with some research beforehand, you can figure out a way to create the position that is closest to perfection for you! Find out what type of people perform the work that you aim to do, the type of training required and the like. Thus, you can minimize negative surprises by knowing how to adjust your expectations – *ahead of time*.

In researching your potential pathway, be honest and be thorough in evaluating *how long* it may take for you to reach your personal goals. It is vital to evaluate as accurately as possible the investment of money, energy and time required of you on the road ahead. For example, it may take a good *fifteen years* of humble living after finishing high school before you start reaping the financial benefits that you envisioned (e.g., **4** years of college + **4** years of medical school + **2** years of residency + **5** years of building up a private practice). For some, the sacrifice is worth it. For others, it is not. Simply put, the more that you invest into researching your career choices, the better your chances of not tiring too early due to over-inflated expectations. Prepare ye for the long, winding road!

No Bones about It:

If **TIME IS MONEY**, then few people can afford to waste both. Time spent on research now may save you time spent on regrets later.

Testing

Furthermore, if you wish to pursue a profession with a definite career path, why wait to prepare? For instance, if you know you want to be a doctor or a lawyer, then you should also know that you need to test well for medical or law school entrance examinations (i.e., the MCAT or LSAT). Since you know this fact ahead of time, practice early.

It behooves you to practice your professional entrance examination several times while there is still time to correct your *deficiencies*. Talk to guidance counselors or mentors early on to ensure that you are taking the appropriate classes and are not only on track to graduate, but are also on track to get into your desired professional school.

Realize that professional schools are looking for specific criteria. Researching school profiles and entrance criteria will assist you in planning for your professional school experience. In today's competitive age, your chances for long-term success will be reduced if you "wake up" in your second semester of your senior year in college and suddenly decide upon a career path. The more time you have to plan, the better. After all, **luck is the residue of design**. You may not be lucky enough to end up doing what you originally set out to do, but with planning, *deliberate steps will yield more deliberate results.*

No Bones about It:

It takes money to make money - do not be surprised at the need to invest significant sums of money into your certification and/or training process to obtain formal recognition in your field.

Certification

For those of you who bravely dare to venture into the world of professional school, complete with extra years of studying, exorbitant student loans and a *de facto* humble lifestyle, we salute you. However, depending upon whether you want to be a doctor, lawyer, accountant or engineer, now is the time to learn the "rules of engagement." Thanks to federalism, each of our fifty states is its own sovereign with its own set of laws – even though united and organized under a larger federal system. This means that earning a license to practice law, for example, is most often specific to the individual state where you took the bar exam.

Typically, your professional license does not automatically act like an open credit card that can be used freely throughout the land. Thus, procedures regarding licensing, reciprocity and specialization for the state of your choice may impact your overall plan significantly. Even a cursory inspection of the state laws for locations where you would like to live will help you avoid running into any "dead ends."

While you are at it, also research the total cost of obtaining your certification. Since some professional exams and accompanying training courses can be very pricey, become familiar with the costs associated with your professional licensing ahead of time so that you can plan accordingly.

Practical Experiences

Can you say "test drive?" It is important to expose yourself to the practical side of the career you are focused upon. We therefore recommend exploring internship or volunteer opportunities – even though they are non-paying positions – since they will provide you with valuable information and knowledge about a particular trade or industry. Besides, if there is ever a time where you can "afford" not to be paid, it is now. These volunteer experiences will not only enhance your knowledge about an industry, but will also give you the valuable opportunity to meet other professionals in your field.

Through both volunteer and unpaid work opportunities, not only will you obtain hands-on experience in your potential field, but you will also establish a relevant track record for your résumé. Further, since the "cost" of personal time is relatively small early in your career, you are afforded an invaluable opportunity to study the "beautiful warts" that your potential profession contains.

Additionally, practical experiences will better position you to determine whether this profession is really right for you. Otherwise, if you "learn" that you do not like what you are doing at a much later point in your career, it may be too difficult to change courses. Surprises make for good daytime television drama but not when it involves your daily unhappiness and your bi-weekly paycheck.

Now, some of you may say that it is too early to get a "real" job. We say **no way!** You will benefit from early exposure to work environments, "office politics," corporate communication styles and so much more. Think of volunteering as practice or dress rehearsal before your "real" job experiences begin. Yet, all the while you are learning about your craft while being insulated from some of the real pressures associated with "real" job performances.

Learning the market through unpaid experiences will also help you decide if you really want to start your own business in this field down the road. Although most magazine articles profiling up-and-coming entrepreneurs often gloss over this point, owning your own business can be extremely stressful. Since owning your own business can be a very demanding affair (i.e., managing people, managing problems and managing other people's problems), it is best to "test" out the market as early as possible.

Role Model/Mentor

NEWS FLASH! There is nothing new under the sun! Find out who is doing what you want and make the effort to contact them so that you can learn from them. If lucky, you may broker a formal relationship with this person and elevate your learning process even more. If you cannot find someone that is willing to let you observe them from close range, then designate a virtual mentor and observe their methods from afar.

Try studying the work product, writings and achievements of a successful individual in your field. Although you may not interact directly with them, you can still benefit by studying an **experienced and successful** individual in your field from afar. Needless to say, reflecting on their life decisions will help you make better decisions about your career.

No Magic Here:

Keys to an Effective Career Plan
→*Research*
→*Certification*
→*Practical experiences*
→*Testing*
→*Role model/mentor*

ASK YOUR FOLKS

Find out whether or not their current employment position was the result of choice or chance. Would they do anything different?

REARVIEW REVIEW

An Innocent Enough Question

☑ *Inquire what you want to do when you "grow up."*

But, What to Do?

☑ *Why wait? Brainstorm your work options now.*

Job vs. Career

☑ *Understand the difference between existing vs. living.*

CEO of YOU, Inc.

☑ *Know your interests, understand your worth.*

Working Double-Time

☑ *Plan on parallel paths to propel professional success.*

Work in Progress

☑ *Researching your role will help you define your route.*

CONNECT THE DOTS

>> *First, try listing three occupations that you can see yourself performing. Next, list at least three specific steps you need to take to secure these positions (aside from "study hard in school").*

>> *For the three occupations, list the type of certification required for each (if any).*

>> *Lastly, make contact with at least one person in each field that you listed above. Figure out what new information they can provide you about the occupation itself.*

CHAPTER 2:
EDUCATION

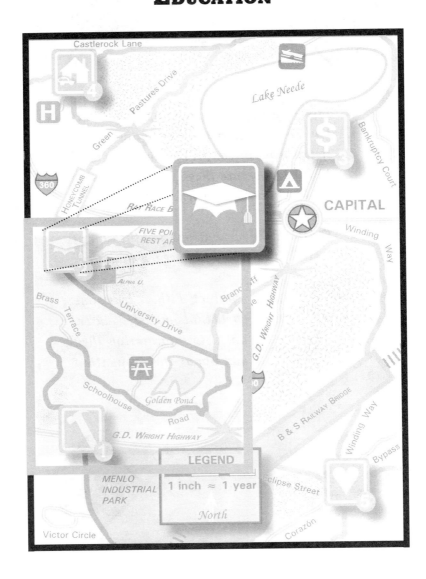

THE ROAD AHEAD

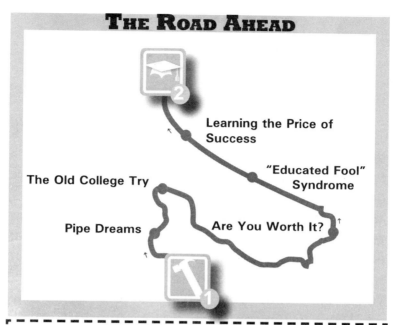

The Old College Try

Learning the Price of
Success

"Educated Fool"
Syndrome

Pipe Dreams   Are You Worth It?

Our next *Decision Point* is **Education**. Your aim should be to pursue a specific education with – but only with specific career goals in mind.

At **Pipe Dreams** we start with the understanding that you will make a living based upon specialized knowledge.

With **The Old College Try**, we acknowledge that while college is not for everyone, we nonetheless recommend it as a good place to start.

At **Are You Worth It?** we make the point that since education is priceless, do approach it as a quality investment.

However, at **"Educated Fool" Syndrome**, we learn that a formal education is a means, but by no means the only means to achieve your goals.

Finally, at **Learning the Price of Success** we encourage you to research both the tangible and intangible costs associated with pursuing a higher education.

CHAPTER TWO
Learning the Road

COURSE PREVIEW

Now that we have considered what we wish to do with our life's energy in *Chapter 1: Career*, we have to carve out a path to these professional goals. Hence, our next stop is **Education**. Why stop at Education *after* stopping at Career? We know some of you are presently asking "Doesn't one usually require an education *before* they decide upon a career?" No! To reiterate the point made in *Chapter 1: Career*, it behooves you to think about your career *first* so that you know what specific direction your future education needs to take. This way, you can make more informed decisions about your education, rather than purely relying upon an "educated guess."

Education is also the next stop for one simple reason: in this society, people will pay you a premium for what you know – especially if you know "it" better than anyone else. In other words, you will be rewarded for your unique expertise. In order to discern how much of an expert you are, one factor future employers or clients will take into consideration is where and how you learned your craft or skill. Thus, you should consider your "higher" education (i.e., beyond high school) and the quality thereof very seriously.

PIPE DREAMS

Did you ever hear the story about the woman who called the Plumber to unclog the pipes in her house? Her in-laws were coming to visit in two days, but the toilet and shower in the guest room were not working properly. She then called the first plumber listed in the phone book over to her house. After hearing a description of the problem, the Plumber surveyed the scene, listened very intently to the inner-workings of the pipes, and abruptly exclaimed "Here!"

The startled woman watched as the Plumber whipped out a small hammer and curtly tapped the pipes before informing her that he was done. The relieved woman thanked the Plumber profusely stating that upon receipt, she would promptly pay the bill since he had saved the day. The Plumber assured the woman he would send an invoice and then left.

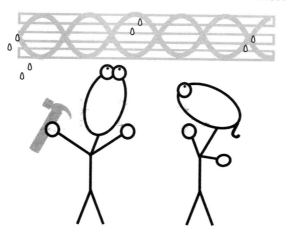

The next week, the woman received the bill in the mail. However, instead of paying, she called the Plumber to complain because she received an invoice for $1,000.00. "I saw the whole thing," she exclaimed. "All you did was tap the pipes!" The Plumber patiently replied, "True – the labor involved in tapping the pipes was only worth $50. However, *knowing where to tap the pipes* was worth $950!"

True to her word, the woman promptly paid the invoice. Now, after hearing this story you might think "Yeah, right!" But our reply is "Yes, that's right!" The moral of the story is that if you "know your pipes" inside and out, people will pay you a hefty premium for that knowledge.

THE OLD COLLEGE TRY

After deciding upon a field, you will need to obtain some type of expert training. Whether you need guidance selecting a profession or developing your expertise within your profession, we recommend college as an excellent starting point.

While college is certainly not for everyone, depending upon what you want to do, it may be highly recommended or even *required*. For instance, if you wish to become a "Highly Qualified Teacher" in one of our nation's public schools under the *No Child Left Behind Act*, then in addition to state-certification, you will need a college degree. Period. Or, if you wish to become a medical doctor, a college degree is a prerequisite before gaining entrance into medical school. This is where doing some research and preliminary planning will help you discern what your future educational needs may be.

Plus, as you recall in *Chapter 1: Career*, typically the more elevated and specific training you have, the better positioned you will be to sell your knowledge or charge for your time at premium market rates. Recall, that as CEO of YOU, Inc., you have to invest in education whether you intend to work for someone else or work for yourself. The key is figuring out the type of "education" required to fulfill your goals (e.g., classes, trainings, jobs, etc.).

No Bones about It:

If you want to be recognized for your skill and expertise, you have to educate yourself on mastering your craft and becoming an expert in your trade.

So when we talk about obtaining "an education" in this chapter, we generally refer to the educational training required to competently charge people for your services. Whether the training occurs within a university setting or elsewhere is up to you.

Please note that a *university* differs from a *college* in that undergraduate, graduate *and* professional degrees are awarded by a university whereas a college typically only offers undergraduate degrees. Nonetheless, our practical pointers equally apply to both experiences. Depending upon whether we are discussing colleges or universities at the time, feel free to substitute the type of institution that is most relevant to your roadmap.

Practically speaking: **not all colleges and universities are created equal**. Generally speaking, colleges are smaller in size, have more specialized coursework, lower student to teacher ratios, and have concentrated campuses. Universities on the other hand, are much larger in size – both in population and physical area, have broader course options and larger classes. In deciding upon your institution, it will be incumbent upon you to prioritize your top choices based upon what suits you best.

While college is often your first step in acquiring elevated training, we readily acknowledge that the collegiate experience does not automatically translate into success for all who attend. Even still, if (after consulting with your folks) you decide college *is* for you, take time to focus on what it truly means to obtain a quality education. Specifically, when thinking about higher education, contemplate the following factors – *before* making your selection:

Academic Requirements

Different colleges have different standards. Even if attending college is a bit far off from where you currently stand, we suggest a basic investigation of general admission requirements to help expose and familiarize yourself with the application process. The more you know early on, the more comfortable your decision-making process should become. For starters, the coursework you select now has a direct impact on your future college choices. So, you and your guidance counselor should consider mapping out a specific course load for you based upon your future career aspirations (e.g., AP courses in certain fields or courses with college credit).

No Bones about It:

If you wish to attend to graduate or professional school, why wait to start practicing the entrance examinations (e.g., MCAT, LSAT, GRE, GMAT)? Practice makes perfect!

Accordingly, the courses that you select now may well differ if you plan to study medicine as opposed to journalism. Nonetheless, the more of an idea you have about your course of study, the better. These same planning principles apply to college undergraduates contemplating the next step either to graduate or professional school.

Another important consideration is taking time to familiarize yourself with the standard entrance examinations (i.e., PSAT, SAT, ACT, LSAT, GMAT, MCAT, etc.). These admissions tests are significant in that they are used by universities to measure your achievement and ability to achieve. Your scores in conjunction with your grades will sketch out a picture of you as a student. One of the most important pieces of advice is that you need to expose yourself *early and often* to these tests. Psst! Just in case someone told you the opposite, at this time we would like to share with you a secret tip: **the test scores do matter**. Yet, as much as good test scores on a standardized examination reflect individual achievement, good test scores also reflect familiarity with the exam itself.

Watch for Bull:

The scores for your college, graduate or professional school entrance examinations don't matter – yeah right! If that's the case, why do you think they keep score?

Grades will obviously be an important factor in the admission process, too. Thus, special focus should be given to your in-school achievement and academic performance. Pushing yourself for the **"A"** as opposed to "settling" for a **"B+"** may make a difference if you know that you are competing for a spot at one of the nation's more competitive universities. Conversely, if you have an action-packed schedule with sports, community service *and* student government responsibilities, then the **"B+"** may suffice *if* this one course is not directly applicable to your ultimate goals. Now of course, our official position is to shoot for the **"A+"** every time, but you want to *work smart* in addition to *working hard* for your grades.

Lastly, take a look at what schools admire and value in their ideal student population. Needless to say, if you have received any award or special recognition for some achievement – that should be highlighted too! Since your extra-curricular activities and personal interests will also play a part in the admissions process, plan to spend your free time wisely.

The question now becomes, why did you select the school that you did? Is it because your parents went there? Is it because it is the closest one to home? Is it because your best friend told you about it? Is it because it is located in a city and climate that you like? Is it because you saw their football or basketball team on TV? Is it solely because they offered you the best financial aid package? Or is it because they have a unique academic program that is of special interest to you?

The truth is, often times people select schools for reasons that have nothing to do with their *end goal* of pursuing a defined career. Accordingly, we urge you to consider the *totality* of the package (e.g., institutional legacy, financial aid package, expected coursework, geographic location, etc.) so that a single reason does not unduly influence your decision.

Watch for Bull:

National academic rankings are for administrators' bragging rights, not potential students. Stay focused on your goals; the "best" school simply may not be the best fit for your roadmap.

Conversely, it is also a good idea from the onset to be clear on the requirements necessary for you to graduate. After you get into college, the first question you need to answer (besides "where do they make good pizza around here?") is *how to get out of college?* To successfully graduate and "get out" of college, you need to make sure that you obtain the type of academic and social support necessary to maximize your collegiate experience.

Many movies and television shows portray college as a time of very little responsibility, a time where students can explore and "find themselves" with very little homework or with little need for extended studying – and yet everything "works out" in the end. Let's pretend this scenario does not apply to you and that you will need a prepared plan *prior* to your arrival that will help you stay on track to graduate *on time*.

Learning Community

Upon making your choice, it is essential to keep in mind that you are not merely attending a college or university, but rather an institution. An institution means much more than the words emblazoned on your sweatshirt – *it represents a culture* and in some cases a philosophy. Realize also that you are tapping into an existing network that will expand your horizons according to the sphere of its influence. This is why so many people make such a fuss about attending Ivy League or "name brand" schools.

Real-Road Crossing

Intersection: Capital + Education
Universities are abundant with resources relevant to your goals. Get your money's worth by familiarizing yourself with offices, departments, programs, staff and faculty who are there to assist you.

Some schools, however, which have less of a national reputation, may have more influence in their immediate geographic region. Thus, it is vitally important to consider selecting a college or university that is known for its challenging and rigorous training environment or that has access to surrounding businesses and resources in *your desired field*. The bottom line is that you will need to consider the institution's sphere of influence on your ultimate career goals when deciding on schools both within and outside of your current community.

Another consideration is learning more about the respected professors and professionals in your field. In other words, you will need to familiarize yourself with the "hot" topics as well as the culture of your profession. The sooner you learn the "lingo" and the "secret code words" particular to your field, the better off you will be in solidifying your position along the inside track.

It is also essential that you take stock of your educational prospects *outside of the classroom*. Specifically, think in terms of the type of the professional community located near your future institution. In order to land great internships or mentors that will catapult you further into your industry, you will need access to these businesses and mentoring opportunities. For example, going to school in South Dakota may not be the most practical option if you have your heart set on becoming a Hollywood screenwriter. On the other hand, going to school in the Los Angeles area will place you closer to "the action" and will provide you with more opportunities for a lucky break. Recall, **luck is the residue of design**. So, you have the power to design your *Roadmap to Success* today!

Real-Road Crossing

Intersection: Career + Education
Depending upon where you would like to ultimately work, look to get your education from the same geographic area as well.

In sum, make sure to know what communal aspects you are looking for from your college or university *ahead of time*. Collegiate community life is such an important quality because your external learning environment should compliment the growth taking place inside of the classroom. So, for your benefit, make a list of the important attributes that you want out of your learning community. Once you identify specifically what you are looking for, it will become easier to seek it out – and find it!

Leadership Opportunities

The collegiate experience will provide several opportunities for you to provide guidance and direction to others. For example, there will be numerous clubs, organizations, athletic teams and teaching assistant opportunities at your school. Thus, you will have ample opportunity to develop personally as a leader throughout the time that you are involved in these extra-curricular activities.

Exploring these leadership opportunities are essential because you will have the opportunity to practice your ability to plan, organize and lead your peers in one way or another. Such a challenging experience will prove beneficial in the "real world" as well. Whether you coordinate activities, develop team goals or facilitate meetings – the skills employed and garnered as a leader will be of the utmost use to you as you manage your successful business (e.g., CEO of YOU, Inc.), or any other position.

Whether you ultimately decide to work for yourself or for others, having leadership skills and the confidence to employ them is absolutely key to your forward progress. Plus, by placing yourself in a leadership position, you will – by necessity – have to expand your circle of contacts. The benefit of networking with new individuals and building new coalitions is that these relationships may eventually prove instrumental for your long-term goals – but only if managed properly. Bear in mind that these relationships do not manage themselves, so as with most things worth having, prepare to invest your money, time and energy into these relationships over the long-term as well.

No Magic Here:

Keys to any Educational Experience
→ *Academic Requirements*
→ *Learning Community*
→ *Leadership Opportunities*

ARE YOU WORTH IT?

College or professional school, no matter how enjoyable, is still a big deal. Blessed is the soul who skates through without having to pay for both. Rare is the soul who only has to pay for one and *then there is you.* Under the theory that **it takes money to make money**, the investment into a college education with hopes of a future payoff can become quite an expensive proposition. In fact, some institutions charge as much as $45,000 a year for the privilege of learning "the classics."

For the sake of argument, however, let's suppose that you do not secure any grants or scholarships and that your parents will be unable to foot that tuition bill. Let's also suppose that in addition to taking out school loans for college that you will have to do so for professional school as well. Now what? Is it time to panic? No. It is time to *plan.*

The tough decision to willingly shoulder potentially hundreds of thousands of dollars in debt is harrowing – especially for aspiring first-generation professionals. Yet, there are a number of opportunities out there for you to discover an entity who will fund your education by way of grant or scholarship. The key is locating these individuals and organizations *ahead of time* and making yourself *marketable* to these organizations.

Recall, you will hardly ever get something for nothing in this **LifeTime**. Scholarship donors are no different. You can find people willing to give you money, just so long as you are able to demonstrate that your interests *coincide* or that your work will further *the donors'* aims or objectives. Must we remind you that it is a big world out there, so do not be discouraged. Some person, institution or organization is willing to help you – you just may not have found them as yet.

If all else fails, there are always loans that can be made available to you. Upon accepting a school loan, however, do not feel guilty, overburdened or overwhelmed – you are making an investment in yourself (think CEO of YOU, Inc.)! The benefit about school loans is that you increase your opportunities for social and economic advancement – *only if* you take advantage of your education.

Bear in mind, the primary risk with school loans is that after finally completing school and after finally landing a job, you still may not make enough to live your desired lifestyle *and repay* back your loan. Still, the key is having a plan in place to make that money back – and then some – *ahead of time.*

No Bones about It:

School loans as a personal investment can be quite expensive. Then again, your education is *priceless.*

While there are no guarantees that you will "make it all back," we submit that **you are worth the risk**. Is it even worth going into debt before turning a profit? Yes, because if managed with purpose and commitment, a college education will expose you to more opportunities for advancement. Yet, in order to receive a "return on your investment," you will not only need to take your educational process seriously, but will also need to use your education wisely.

More important than where you go to college is where you go *after* you finish college. Start now to structure the education you receive (both inside and outside the classroom) against your roadmap. Plan now to eventually profit from the accumulation of your knowledge. Again, this planning process does not guarantee your success, but it enhances your chances.

"EDUCATED FOOL" SYNDROME

One cautionary note as you consider a higher degree – beware of the "educated fool" syndrome. The educated fool syndrome refers to cases where a person is educated on paper but has nothing tangible to show for all of their degrees. Higher education is undoubtedly important since it often represents a viable means for upward mobility – yet, in reality the degree or certificate is only as good as the parchment or paper that it is printed upon. Only your degree **plus a plan of execution** will improve your chances of success, not the degree in and of itself.

Many mistakenly rely solely upon their education to take them places. While we obviously endorse the pursuit of higher education, we also need to forewarn you that success is not promised nor guaranteed merely because you *graduated* with a professional or undergraduate degree (regardless of whether you attended an Ivy League school or not).

Moreover, what you *do not* want to do is graduate from college and then start thumbing through the classified section the next day in search of a job – or worse, move back home with your parents! You know what? While we are at it, put this book down (just for a brief moment, mind you) and grab the classified section of your local newspaper. What type of jobs are you well-suited for? What type of jobs appeal to you?

Which jobs do you currently qualify for? Do you trust these advertisements? What do you think about the starting pay scale? Are you worth more? If so, why? More importantly, how can you prove it? Lastly, will the degree that you are currently seeking prepare you for the jobs you see listed?

In other words, **what you do not want** is to find yourself dressed up in fancy degrees with "no place to go." Trust us, it happens without fail every year: an otherwise bright and talented Young Adult makes an expensive investment in their education, and either "can't" find a job or "settles" for a job that they could have landed without ever having attended college or professional school.

B.S.

M.A.

B.A.

J.D.

PhD

M.D.

M.S.

MBA

In a general sense, all you really need to enter the modern workforce is knowledge of "business phone demeanor," how to perform word processing and surf the internet (you can learn how to make coffee and double-sided copies during your first week on the job). Thus, the key question is, what additional skill can you learn or acquire while in college that will distinguish yourself from the competition in your respective job market?

Conversely, while everyone wants to "get paid" immediately after graduating from college, the question becomes, *what position justifies a high salary with relatively little "real world" experience*? As a Young Adult entering the marketplace, you will have the challenge of facing people older than you who have been working "all of their adult life" to be successful, and here you are, seeking to make more money than they. What justifies paying you more than them? What is it that you know that they do not know? Which tasks can you perform more efficiently? What knowledge can you honestly sell at a higher premium?

Well, the reality is that even though you may have degrees from impressive institutions that cost you plenty of money, time and energy, the financial recognition you seek may not be immediately forthcoming. Therefore, for times like these, it is generally a good idea to continue along a career path that you genuinely find worthwhile. Recall, that by placing job satisfaction before job compensation, your job will be doubly rewarding *if and when* you do "get paid." If you place job compensation before job satisfaction (i.e., "chase the cheese"), you might ask the following questions of yourself:

> >> **I just don't get it. I put in all this "work" in college and took out all of these school loans. How come no one will compensate me according to my projected salary?**
>
> >> **Doesn't anyone understand that I have the degrees to prove that I am worth more?**
>
> >> **Was all of my "education" for naught?**

Not exactly. Get your education. But simply understand that higher education only *increases* your chances of success but *does not guarantee* them.

ASK YOUR FOLKS
Find out whether or not they felt higher education after high school was necessary to prepare them for their current position. Would they do anything different?

REARVIEW REVIEW

Pipe Dreams

☑ *Knowledge is power (and money).*

The Old College Try

☑ *Try it! College may enhance your chances of success.*

Are You Worth It?

☑ *College can be costly, but your education is priceless.*

"Educated Fool" Syndrome

☑ *Learn how to convert your degrees into dividends.*

Learning the Price of Success

☑ *It takes time to make money; research the true costs.*

CONNECT
THE
DOTS

>> *Imagine that you received a full scholarship to each of your top three college choices. Write a two-sentence statement stating why you would attend each school.*

>> *Now, research and write down your intended field of study, the appropriate department, relevant coursework and a professor to serve as your mentor at one of the institutions selected above.*

>> *For your first choice, contact the professor and explain your desire to attend their institution (using the two-sentence statement), and ask for their input about your intended course of study.*

CHAPTER 3:
CAPITAL

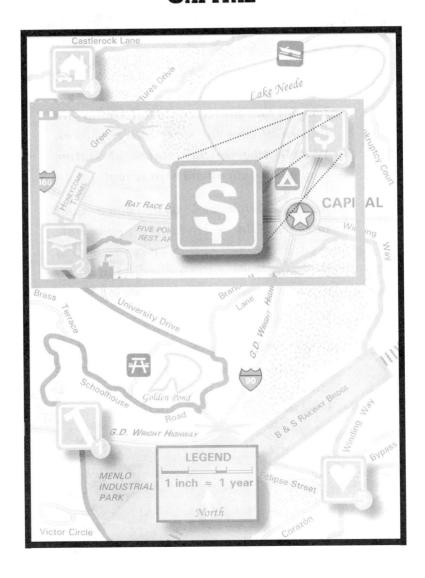

THE ROAD AHEAD

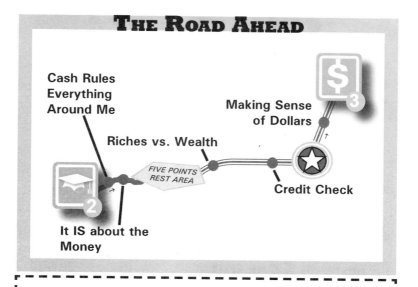

Cash Rules Everything Around Me

Making Sense of Dollars

Riches vs. Wealth

FIVE POINTS REST AREA

Credit Check

It IS about the Money

As we move from **Education** to **Capital**, we look to successfully convert intangible, specialized knowledge into tangible, capital gains.

At **Cash Rules Everything Around Me** we discuss the function of money in our increasingly commercial and capitalistic society.

But at **It IS about the Money** we form a money-making mindset not fueled by greed, but rather driven by a passion for success.

At **Riches vs. Wealth** we highlight the difference between assets and liabilities. Specifically, we evaluate how to value the significant material purchases that you will likely make on the road ahead.

At **Credit Check**, we advocate controlling your credit before it controls you.

Lastly, at **Making Sense of Dollars,** we further emphasize the importance of knowing the price you will pay for "getting paid."

CHAPTER THREE
FINANCING YOUR TRIP

COURSE PREVIEW

Understanding capital and how it operates in our society will help you understand how much money you will need to get to your ultimate destination. Fuel is not cheap these days, so if you want to go far, you will have to repeatedly fill up the tank along the way. Quite simply, you need a plan for creating and dealing with your current and future finances. For this reason, our next stop is **Capital**.

Once you work to acquire money, how will you make it work for you? How will you invest, save or spend it? How will you make it grow? The intent of this chapter is to encourage you to start seeking answers to these questions *now*. Think of money as a **tool** that if used correctly, will come in quite handy for the construction of your long-term plans.

The fact of the matter is, money is embedded within our openly commercial and capitalistic society. **Capital** is a *Decision Point* on our roadmap because depending upon how much you have, it can literally afford you additional opportunities for success. The *best things* in life are for free. OK. Problem is, *everything else* costs money. So the challenge is, how do you plan to make money, use it, and then make some more?

CASH RULES EVERYTHING AROUND ME

Again, money is largely a tool used to leverage tangible objects and intangible services. The obligation to exchange money, however, is not always reflected in a face-to-face consumer transaction where one party pays another for a tangible good or service. In other words, if you reflect on the course of your day and the amount of time you spend engaged in "transactions," you may be surprised to discover the level of commerce that you frequently conduct throughout your day.

For example, when you think "transaction," you may immediately think about buying lunch, purchasing clothes, paying your cell phone bill, filling up the car with gas or sending a package through the mail. However, what about exchanges that may not be quite so obvious? Did you brush your teeth (and floss) today? Well, provided so, did you notice that the "free-flowing," cool, crisp, mountain-spring water that came cascading through your bathroom spigot was not exactly "free"?

Although you may not think of this transaction in direct terms of money, be advised that this daily ritual does in fact cost you money. The amount of water your family uses each month is recorded, measured, and converted into a price that your folks must pay as part of a regular utility bill. Essentially, all that we do costs money in some way, shape or form. Thus, because we live in a capitalistic society, it behooves you to become "money-minded."

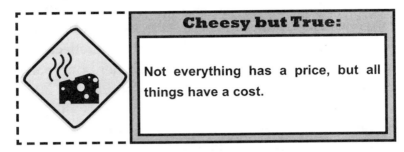

Cheesy but True:

Not everything has a price, but all things have a cost.

The million-dollar question thereby becomes: since everyone has to pay for nearly everything they do, are there any opportunities for you to participate in and profit from these transactions as well?

Some people choose a job because "that's where the money is." Still, the ultimate challenge is choosing a task that you not only like, but can simultaneously profit from as well. So, do yourself a favor and begin thinking about the type of **Career** that will meet your "needs" – financial as well as personal. Caviar, designer jeans, penthouses and Learjets aside, basics such as food, clothing, shelter and transportation must be included in your calculus. Now is a good time to start thinking practically about the salary you really need to support the lifestyle you really want.

Again, let us be clear: **you NEED to make money in your LifeTime**. The funny thing is, very few people are willing to openly admit this. Many people state that they only want a "simple life" or that "they don't want any money." If you are all about the simple life, then put this book down and let the rest of us materialistic capitalists talk amongst ourselves. Or better yet, the next time you get something to eat at a restaurant, ask yourself whether money does not matter when it is time to settle your bill.

The bottom line is that money represents **power, opportunity** and **choice** in our society. Many people who have considerable influence in our society "coincidentally" have considerable amounts of money. Yet, it is no coincidence that when choosing among travel fares (e.g., first class or coach), selecting a restaurant, or deciding upon clothing styles, *more money* usually means *more options* for the activities that you typically engage. High capital accumulation influences the variety and type of choices available to you primarily through the twin luxuries of *disposable income* and *leisure time* – luxuries that are not to be taken for granted since they are deceptively difficult to afford (time is money, remember?).

Money also ensures financial stability. So when we advocate adopting a money-minded perspective on life at an early stage, it is not for purely materialistic reasons. People want money because people *need* money – and you are no different. While money may be seen as a superficial indicator of "success," it definitely has a clear and valued place in our society that most people will and do in fact recognize. Plainly put, in our capitalistic society, capital is absolutely *necessary* for survival. So, in order to survive according to the standards that you set for yourself, you will need a plan of action to secure enough capital to comfortably finance your goals.

IT IS ABOUT THE MONEY

Regardless of how an individual defines success, an ever-present goal will always be to acquire *and maintain* a certain level of financial success. Whether you work with a multi-national corporation, non-profit organization, small business or sole proprietorship, your success will in part be measured by monetary gain. In addition to your individual goals, the goal of each and every organization or entity you work with is prosperity and growth. Of course, this is all a very nice way of saying, *it IS about the money!*

So, the next time you hear "it's not about the money," please pay close attention to who said it and the context of their statement. Also notice whether the financial status of the orator is stable and secure. For instance, do they have assets? Homes? Fancy cars? No uniform rules apply here, but if the answer is "yes," then you can see how a more financially secure lifestyle might *afford* the speaker the luxury of saying that "it is not about the money."

Watch for Bull:

It's not about the money. Ideally, this altruistic phrase should ring true. Yet, in order to practically finance your lifestyle at any level, money is required. Whether you spend your money or that of other people, money is required to survive.

What we also wish to make clear is that financial stability operates on a relative scale. Thus, you will likely never cease in your search for money to advance your standard of living. Let us be clear: even people with money want and need to make more money! Depending on your current level of financial wealth, others may see you as being comfortable although you still may have individual needs and goals that remain unfulfilled by your own standards. Regardless of your status, only you truly know your financial situation. Do not feel ashamed of your pursuit for capital. Just feel ashamed if whilst in pursuit of capital, you violate moral, ethical or legal standards of conduct. Other than that, you are fully justified in your *quest to survive in this society* and to do so comfortably.

Make a difference in the world and make some money, but *do not* make any pretenses about it. And whatever you do, please do not needlessly repeat the phrase: "I'm not going to change with the money." **The hay you won't!** Once you have additional financial options, everything changes – isn't that the whole point? Practically speaking, you want the additional choices, opportunities and stability in your life that more money affords you.

Again, do not be ashamed. You want to make money because you *need* to make money. Moreover, capital is an essential ingredient in affording yourself the lifestyle that you desire. Just say out loud what you and everybody else already knows to be true: *it IS about the money.* Embrace this concept now in your quest for success. In other words, **plan now to profit later!**

RICHES vs. WEALTH

While attaining financial stability in order to maintain your desired standard of living is important, you also want to consider ways to build your wealth over time. Wealth is established by building and amassing **assets**. But what exactly is an asset? Generally speaking, an asset is personal or real property that appreciates in value over time. Common examples include:

1. real estate
2. jewelry
3. stocks/bonds
4. antiques
5. profitable business enterprise

All of these above-listed items can grow in value over time and are generally regarded as appreciating assets. Notice however, what type of items that did NOT make the list:

> **1. *expensive shoes***
> **2. *expensive clothes***
> **3. *high-tech electronic equipment***
> **4. *fancy cars***
> **5. *"bling-bling"***

The above list represents depreciating assets – meaning that the more you use them, the more they decrease in value. Thus, when purchasing any "big-ticket" item (i.e., item perceived of great value), you want to reflect on the actual value, quality and long-term use of the item.

Assets also refer to those tangible items that translate into a recognized value *by creditors* (e.g., real estate, antiques, stocks and bonds, etc.) Unfortunately, the car that you are leasing or are still financing with monthly payments is not an asset – even though you "bought" it with your own money. In fact, any remaining amount that you have left on a financed car is a negative debt you must pay before realizing any monetary gain. Further, with continued use, a car depreciates steadily in market value over time, despite its "invaluable" status in your eyes.

Since **assets + liabilities = net worth**, the key to building wealth is maximizing your assets and minimizing your liabilities. Liabilities often take the form of items that lose value or are of negative value. Items of negative value are commonly referred to as **debts**, or financial obligations incurred and owed by you to a third party (e.g., credit cards, student loans, mortgage, etc.). Ideally, you will use the capital you earn to invest into your future as opposed to continuing to pay for the past.

If you bought a house and a car on the same day,

ITEM	PRICE	VALUE IN 5 YEARS
🏠	$250,000	$275,000 = asset
🚗	$50,000	$25,000 = liability

Assets **A**ppreciate in value

Liabilities **L**ose value

<u>NOTE:</u> *In our view, depreciating assets qualify as liabilities since they both have the same effect on your overall wealth status. Check with an accountant to accurately assess your situation.*

In any event, at this stage of your life, you may have very few significant assets and/or liabilities in your financial portfolio. However, there is no time like the present to start understanding the concept of money and how money operates and functions in our society. Similarly, in starting off your quest for "a successful life," proper management of both your personal finances and credit early on will help you tremendously when it is time to build your wealth.

CREDIT CHECK

Presuming that one day you will be gainfully employed and making money, we can now focus on your future need to establish a good credit history. A good credit history is important because when purchasing a "big-ticket" item, you will need credit to finance the purchase *if you cannot pay outright with cash.* Financing requires borrowing other people's money. So, whenever others consider giving you money – especially if they do not otherwise know you – they need to assess whether they will ever get their money back. It follows that before people do business with you (or YOU, Inc.), they want to know whether they can trust you. Hence, the better your credit rating, the lower their risk and the greater their trust in you. In any event, your ability to leverage credit generally relies upon the following factors:

1. *debt to income ratio*
2. *credit worthiness*
3. *available assets*

Your ***debt to income ratio (DTI)***, as the percentage of your gross monthly income used to pay past debts, is a tool that creditors use to determine the status of your financial well-being. Thus, if and when you use your credit card, form the habit of using it only as a substitute for *cash that you already have.* Pay off your monthly statements **on time** and **in full** and then, before you know it, you will have a whistle-clean credit history in addition to a low DTI that you can leverage for serious capital "down the road." A low DTI will undoubtedly shape the future direction of your overall roadmap (e.g., opening your own practice, starting a small business or buying a house).

Cheesy but True:

Life without money is literally "no funds." Pay credit card debts in full now, or you won't be able to pay later.

Honestly, there is no such thing as a "pizza emergency," or an "emergency sale" at the mall. For this reason, choose your debt wisely since a few hundred dollars here and there will quickly balloon into a five-figure note that can hang over your head for years. Trust us, once you find yourself in the "daily grind" working full-time with your monthly expenses already accounted for, you will find that you only have enough to make minimum payments on your debts. While this minimum payment strategy maintains the status quo for you, it also maintains a smile on the faces of your credit card companies. Why? Well, minimum payments are more detrimental in the long-run because you end up paying well more than the original amount borrowed over the life of the debt.

With respect to **credit worthiness**, it follows that whenever a significant purchase is involved (as with a car or a home), expect for the proprietor to "pull your credit" or review your credit history – especially when you cannot pay the full price in cash. Credit checks will also occur when you attempt to rent or lease an office space or apartment. Additionally, whenever you apply for new credit cards, seek to transfer existing credit card balances or attempt to take out new lines of credit, your creditors will pull your credit again. With so many people looking to pull your credit on so many different occasions, it behooves you to have a good credit rating!

When we say "line of credit," we also refer to those promotional offers from furniture or electronic stores that promise you no payments until some future date. If you read the fine print, you will learn that such an offer is made to everyone so that more customers come to the store. However, the transaction is only finalized with those who prove *creditworthy*.

As far as ***available assets*** are concerned, typically, the more you have, the more you shall receive. Your lenders or creditors often like to designate available assets of yours as collateral or security against a loan. This way, if for some unfortunate reason you are unable to satisfy your obligation to pay, your creditor or lender still gets paid through the liquidation of your assets. Thus, the benefit of acquiring and amassing assets is that not only do they individually increase in value, but they potentially increase your credit worthiness by minimizing your classification as a major credit risk.

Ironically, the less you appear to need money, the more that other people's money will be made available to you.

No Magic Here:

3 Key Elements of Credit
→*Debt to income ratio*
→*Credit worthiness*
→*Available assets*

MAKING SENSE OF DOLLARS

Another key component of financial stability is understanding your current financial situation in *precise terms.* You need to understand your money in order to understand how you will make your money work for you. For example, you probably should not budget your lifestyle based upon your stated salary because **you always take home less than your officially listed salary**. The "hidden" costs of living are often neglected by aspiring young employees who account for their earnings before their checks are cashed.

For example, say you are supposed to go shopping on a budget. Typically, you see product "A" on sale for **$99.95** and you say quietly to yourself "Oh, that's only a hundred bucks." In theory, you are close.

Technically, you are wrong. Unless you live in Alaska, Delaware, Montana, New Hampshire or Oregon, then you have to pay sales tax baby! In California, that can run you as high as **7.25%**! The bottom line is that despite the **$99.95** price tag, you will typically leave the store paying more than a hundred dollars. Does it make a difference? Maybe. Maybe not. But this optimistic math also works in the reverse.

Say you are slated to receive a **$50,000.00** salary. In your excitement, you whip out your calculator and deduce that you are slated to receive **$4,166.00** on a monthly basis. Then, you start calculating what you are going to do with all of that money. The only thing is, you are not going to receive or be able to legally keep all of that money. First, you have to account for taxes since your chief "partners in crime" will be your federal, state and local governments. Many of these taxes in addition to health care deductions and 401(k) or 403(b) contributions are taken off the top. Then, you have to add up your essential expenditures (i.e., what it costs you to stay "in business" as CEO of YOU, Inc.) – including but not limited to, commuting costs, lodging, wardrobe, cell phone, etc.

Alas! Do not forget that you must also account for your discretionary expenses. You also have to handle basic living expenses such as dry-cleaning, utilities, furniture, food, etc. Additional debts and obligations, which may include credit card debt or school loan debt, should also be included in this analysis.

Now, all of a sudden, that **$50,000** may not appear to be as large a number as originally anticipated. Further, after satisfying all of your expenses, you may not be accruing as much capital on a monthly basis as you would like. This optimistic math makes you a prime candidate for "alligator economics." This term refers to the phenomena where the value of one's wages over time stay relatively constant while one's expenses steadily increase. Refer to the graph below, where wages (represented by the lower straight line) hold steady, while expenses (represented by the upper squiggly line) rise like an alligator's upper jaw.

ALLIGATOR ECONOMICS

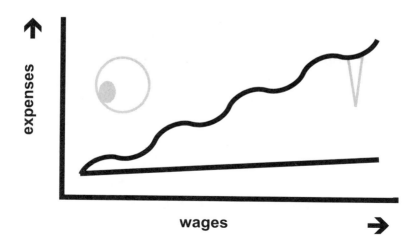

Most unsuspecting victims of alligator economics are lulled to sleep by their dreams of "out-working" their financial woes and by clearing the slate once they hit the jackpot or receive a giant windfall. Then they awake to find themselves squarely in the middle of the *Rat Race* where the "daily grind" is so time-consuming that it is difficult to *make enough money* to fix their financial condition.

We simply wish to alert you to this phenomenon beforehand. When costs increase but income remains constant (or – gulp! – decreases), people are more vulnerable to over-extend themselves on credit, and the *Rat Race* beckons once again. Therefore, in the land of alligator economics, many people think that they are living on their own, when in actuality they are living on borrowed money (and time). This false sense of **"in-debt-pendence"** leads many into believing that the lifestyle they live is their own. Unfortunately, these same individuals often forget that living on borrowed money comes at a hefty monthly premium.

Thus, it is vitally important to understand many of the concepts articulated in this chapter. In sum, (no pun intended), we endeavor to enlighten you about the prominent functions of money in our capitalistic society. While many may claim money is not the focal point of their existence, being financially stable is necessary not only to survive on a daily basis, but also to achieve your desired lifestyle. Most importantly, understanding money concepts (*assets* and *liabilities, debt management* and *credit*) and how to use them to your advantage will not only help you finance your dreams, but will also help maintain and manage an existence built on wealth that can be passed on from generation to generation.

Lastly, a thorough understanding of **Capital** will help you successfully navigate the daily demands of your financial situation. Here, we encourage its accumulation since an increase in financial stability will likely afford you higher levels of independence and autonomy. More specifically, **Capital** is an important tool that can stall progress in its absence and fuel progress when in abundance. Be sure to check your *Roadmap to Success* to see how much fuel you need – *ahead of time*.

ASK YOUR FOLKS
Do they consider themselves "financially secure"? If not, what would it "cost" them to achieve that status in terms of money, energy and time?

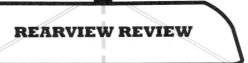

REARVIEW REVIEW

Cash Rules Everything Around Me

☑ *Money is the language we speak. Become fluent.*

It IS about the Money

☑ *A money-making mindset IS what you need!*

Riches vs. Wealth

☑ *Understand and evaluate your assets and liabilities.*

Credit Check

☑ *Control your credit before it controls you.*

Making Sense of Dollars

☑ *Know how to both attain AND maintain your capital.*

 **CONNECT THE DOTS**

>> *See how long you can go without spending any money (or incurring any monetary costs). Is this exercise even practical for everyday living? Of course not! This means noble aspirations aside, you will need to learn how to make money if you plan to survive and not get stuck in the* **Rat Race.**

>> *Ask your folks for a credit card statement. Read all of the fine print on the back, then explain the term "APR" to someone else in three sentences or less.*

>> *Find out what the acronym "FICA" represents and what it means for financial planning.*

CHAPTER 4:
POSSESSIONS

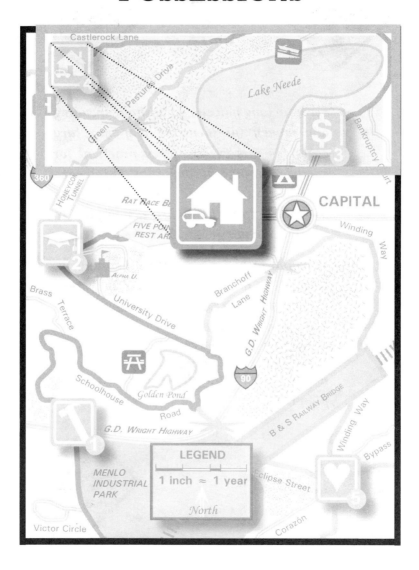

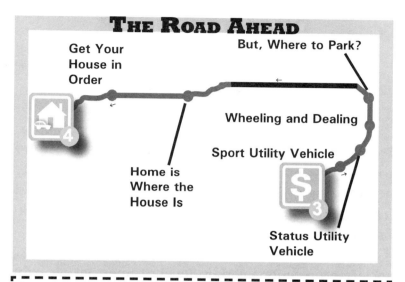

THE ROAD AHEAD

Get Your House in Order

But, Where to Park?

Wheeling and Dealing

Sport Utility Vehicle

Home is Where the House Is

Status Utility Vehicle

As we go from **Capital** to **Possessions** we talk practically about two "big-ticket" items that will require a significant investment of your money, energy and time during your journey to success:

→Car →**Car** →Car →Car →Car →Car

→House →**House** →House →House →House →House

At **Sport Utility Vehicle** and **Status Utility Vehicle** we start with the understanding that when you purchase your car, you must balance your needs against your wants.

Next with **Wheeling and Dealing**, we impart some practical pointers about leasing versus financing a new car.

But, Where to Park? is a discussion about the value of investing into a home.

At **Home is Where the House Is**, we encourage you to reflect on your roadmap while scouting the perfect location to build your dream house.

Finally, at **Get Your House in Order**, we review the accompanying expenses required to maintain these two valuable possessions.

CHAPTER FOUR
SIGNS OF SUCCESS

COURSE PREVIEW

Our next *Decision Point* on the roadmap is **Possessions**. When we say possessions, we refer to two key material possessions that are generally accepted signs that one has attained success: a car and a house (Sorry! You are on your own when it comes to receiving advice on how to nab a flat-screen TV).

Quite simply, *purchasing* a car or a home in our society represents a certain level of financial security since they require significant investments of both time and money. In fact, many people work their whole lives to make these purchases! Thus, their inclusion in your overall success plan should not be underestimated.

The two items featured in this chapter warrant special consideration above other possessions because not only do they serve practical daily functions, but they can also dramatically affect the direction of your roadmap. We now address the utility and value of these two items with several practical pointers in mind.

SPORT UTILITY VEHICLE

For our purposes, we generally classify a car as a liability. Technically, it is an asset, albeit a *depreciating asset*. Why? Well, a car purchase functions as a liability in that you continue to pay for an object that is steadily losing its value. Even if someone gave you a car as a gift outright, the car still loses value (or depreciates) with use over time (see pages 76 or 98 for illustrations).

Although a car is a depreciating asset, we recognize the practical utility of a car for three essential reasons: 1) a car provides increased access to your surroundings, 2) it heightens your independence and 3) a car may become highly instrumental to your professional endeavors or personal business.

Increased Access

It practically goes without saying that an automobile literally opens up the road to you. Simply stated, owning a car provides a broader range of options not available to you if you were completely dependent upon public transportation or upon the goodwill of others to ferry you about.

Heightened Independence

A car is also important since its possession will help facilitate control of your personal schedule. By having your own means of transportation, you are able to directly control your *time* and decide when and where you have to get going. Compare this dynamic to relying on the "sometimes" unreliable public transportation system or goodwill of others.

Professional Function

Lastly, acquiring a vehicle may be necessary for you to earn a living. For example, if you wish to make a living selling real estate, then you will need to have increased access to various locations within a certain geographic space as well as keep a highly personalized and fluid schedule. As such, a car can mean so much more than basic transportation.

If, as the real estate agent, you are meeting a client to purchase a home and hop off a bus to meet the client, you may shake the confidence of this person. Specifically, the client may feel insecure about making a large financial investment with the aid of a person who *at least superficially*, does not appear to have much access to capital. Not to mention, transporting yourself to the sixth or seventh home site may prove to be a logistical nightmare if you are limited to the local bus route and schedule.

Practically speaking, if you go into business for yourself as a private contractor (i.e., an independent plumber), it will be essential to have reliable transportation equipped to tote around your necessary tools and supplies. Possession of a car in this instance allows for better control of the means of your production. Additionally, if you plan correctly, you can lease a car for your business and potentially defray part of the vehicle's expenses as a tax write off. However, this may not be the case with you, so check with your accountant first!

No Magic Here:

Keys to a Practical Car Purchase
→ *Increased access*
→ *Heightened independence*
→ *Professional function*

STATUS UTILITY VEHICLE

Cars also serve practical social functions. Most people recognize that they must acquire a car for the aforementioned reasons we just reviewed. However, many people "make a wrong turn" with the *type* of car that they purchase, and saddle themselves down with a vehicle too expensive to manage comfortably. As a result, many find themselves stuck in the midst of the *Rat Race,* trying to maintain payments on a car that is neither practical, nor affordable for their budget.

With respect to the professional function, your situation may dictate that you should invest in a certain type of car in order to maintain a certain social image that is good for business. For instance, in returning to the real estate agent example, if you meet your clients at your office and drive them around to potential sites, doing so in your beat-up "hooptie" may give your clients the wrong impression about the financial vitality of your business. **Success breeds success. People are attracted to success and symbols of success.** If you are in the service industry and the nature of your job requires that people see or interact with your car, then you will want your car to reflect favorably on your personal status – but not at the expense of financially jeopardizing your business.

Outside of the professional function, similar logic applies with social relations. Many people see the car as an extension of themselves and their external image. Naturally, people want to put their "best foot (or wheel) forward" and invest in a high-end vehicle accordingly. Compact disc players, built-in sunroofs, leather seats, voice-activated cell phones, television headsets, computerized directional aids are but a few of the features that many seek when purchasing a car.

Watch for Bull:

Do not fall for the phrase: **"You are what you drive."** Subscribing to this philosophy drives you deeper into debt while on the fast track to the *Rat Race*.

There is nothing wrong with embellishing your automobile with these additional features – in fact some are highly recommended. Yet, these features come at a price, and many find themselves more entrenched in the *Rat Race* because they spend too much on the features and do not spend enough time thinking about what they can truly afford. Taking a moment or pausing to think about the actual necessity, function and affordability of your vehicle will help you plan for the demands associated with maintaining its possession.

WHEELING AND DEALING

We have spent some time addressing the purpose and use of a car in this society. Now, it is time to address the financial options associated with purchasing a car. Well, before "wheeling and dealing" for the smell of a new car, you should first figure out the total cost to you. You essentially have two options: lease or purchase.

Leasing

Leasing a car may have its advantages for a first time car "owner." We use the word owner liberally because the company leasing the car to you will actually own the car and hold legal title to the car. You will just have "possession" of the car. A car lease essentially is a contract for a finite period of time wherein you agree to pay a certain amount each month for the privilege and pleasure of driving and putting gas in the car. Additionally, lease contracts often allow for: 1) a potentially more luxurious car for less per month and 2) a more extensive warranty plan.

Leasing is usually beneficial to companies or businesses. Leasing for purely personal use can become a hidden trap if done with little research. For instance, many leases contain terms outlining the amount of mileage permitted to you during the term of the lease. An inaccurate mileage estimate can and will cost you if the terms of the lease are not completely explained or understood. What may appear to be a benign charge per mile for exceeding the mileage limit can add up rather swiftly into an imposing amount at the end of the lease. In other words, make sure that you ask plenty of questions before signing any contract, let alone a car lease.

Cheesy but True:

If your deal for four wheels does not add up, use your two heels instead and walk away.

Often, people are reluctant to ask questions in situations like these because they do not want to appear "petty," or do not want to give "false impressions" about not having a lot of money. Uh, remember what we discussed in *Chapter 3: Capital*; it IS about the money – namely *your* money that will soon become *their* money! There is no shame in being crystal clear about where your money is going. Since you work hard for your money, make whoever is on the other side of the table work even harder for your money!

Purchasing

If you decide to buy a car, just remember that **purchasing** a car and **owning** a car are two different things. It has been said that car dealers are not in the car business, but that they are really in the *finance* business. If you attempt to buy a car, but cannot afford to pay the total purchase price in cash or credit, then you will more than likely finance (i.e., use your credit to take out a loan to cover the remaining amount of the purchase price). In essence, you have a debt for the balance owed on the car. Title (i.e., ownership) does not pass to you until the total amount of the debt is paid to the financing company. When you finance the purchase of a car, you do not own the car until the last payment is rendered. However, as the *purchaser*, you do have physical possession and use of the car.

DRIVING COSTS UP

Here's why we maintain that cars largely should be thought of as liabilities. Note the following example:

ITEM	PRICE	VALUE IN 2 YEARS	$ OWED
🚗	$25,000	$13,000	$17,000

Let's suppose you purchase and finance a car for $25,000. After two years of payments, you still owe $17,000 on the vehicle. Problem is, due to depreciation, it is only worth $13,000. Congratulations! Now you have a negative equity gap of $4,000. So, if you decide to sell or trade in Car #1 to buy Car #2, then the most that anyone will give or credit you for your $17,000 car is $13,000, since that is its actual value. Psst! Guess what? You still must pay the original owner $4,000 in order to release the title to you before you trade it in.

ITEM	PRICE	EQUITY GAP	$ FINANCED
🚗	$40,000	$4,000	$44,000

Now that you have a FAMILY, you need a bigger car to accommodate your needs. Car #2 means a bigger price tag of $40,000. But guess what? Your $40,000 car has now just cost you $44,000 due to your negative equity gap! Your second dealership will gladly "roll the balance" into your new purchase price. After the compounded interest charges associated with say, a 60-month financing term, you could well end up paying thousands more for your 2nd car!

Assets
ppreciate in value

Liabilities
ose value

If you finance a **brand new car**, it is not an unencumbered asset because it *depreciates* with use over time. *Depreciation* means that a new car loses value beginning with the moment that you drive it off the lot. Unfortunately, no matter the initial price, every car loses significant value from the moment it leaves the car lot. So, the key question here is whether you are willing to pay an additional premium solely for that new car smell? What if you shed the societal pressures of "newer, faster, better" and simply went with what you could afford? What do you have to prove except creditworthiness to your future lenders?

Do your folks own a car? Quiz them. When they say purchasing a car is easy and "not to worry," prompt them to talk about the details of their experience and the transaction itself. As with anything, make sure you do your research before purchasing a very large item.

If you do decide to finance the purchase of a vehicle, whether new or used, try to limit the term to thirty-six months or less – this way, you will own the car outright after three years and can take better advantage of its resale value. As far as monthly payments go, there is no magic here. Typically, the larger the down payment, the lower your monthly payment will be, and vice versa.

As an alternative, for at least your first car, strongly investigate purchasing a used car. You will shoulder an additional "maintenance risk" since you will not know for certain the car's prior history. Yet, you obtain the benefit of someone else absorbing the car's initial – and largest – depreciation hit. While the car will still depreciate while in your possession, it will likely do so at a slower rate relative to the original price that *you paid for it.*

Most used cars do not look beat up and rusty and sputter and spout about the way some early nineteenth century inventions did. If you are wary about stumbling upon a "shady deal," then check with reputable authorized dealers rather than the classified section of your newspaper. But above all things, do yourself a favor and investigate **ALL** possible deals based upon your driving needs *and* budget.

BUT, WHERE TO PARK?

Now that you have a car, where are you going to park it? Probably at the same place where you park your body at the end of a long day. Purchasing a house, however, is so much more than finding a place to sleep. A house demonstrates: 1) credit worthiness if you faithfully pay your mortgage payment monthly, 2) a tangible asset that can appreciate in time as you make improvements and 3) access to the equity necessary to finance personal "projects."

In comparison – you do *not* want to rent an apartment in perpetuity because over the long-term, it is a waste of money. A few more reasons to buy a house are: 1) the interest on mortgage payments now become tax write-offs, 2) you can build equity and potentially profit from your investment upon resale, and 3) you can increase the quality of your lifestyle. Unlike a car which typically depreciates in value, a home typically appreciates in value, allowing for you to **build wealth**.

There are literally thousands of books that adequately cover what you need to look for when purchasing a home. The function of this chapter here is merely to put the idea of purchasing a home on your radar early so that you can think about reviewing those books and becoming more knowledgeable on the topic.

The hardest part about purchasing a home, is securing proper financing. Based upon available credit and **Capital**, you will receive approval for a certain mortgage amount. This amount may increase based upon the amount that you are personally able to contribute (i.e., down payment). So either you save up, or use a gift from someone else to get into the door. *So here is something to think about:* maybe – just maybe – instead of using both of your savings to finance that big wedding, think of something more modest and use that cash for closing costs instead.

Conundrum: How to not throw money away paying rent for an apartment, but still save up cash for a down payment? Excellent question! The sooner you answer it, the better off you will be! Seriously, the short answer is to save up money. But, the key is *when* and *how* do you start saving? Alas! We do not have an immediately easy answer to this imminently challenging question. It goes without saying that the earlier you start planning for this expense, the better off you will be. Even by storing away small amounts now in contemplation of the future, you will nonetheless help the future arrive faster.

We are not going to spend a whole lot of time on all the rigors of sharing an apartment with roommates. True, you can save money if you have roommates, but the pros and cons are for you to decide. The most important matter to consider early on is positioning yourself to purchase a house – especially if you plan to have a family (see *Chapter 5: Companionship*). Even if you do not intend to have a family or spouse, this investment will give you the opportunity to establish yourself financially. Here are a few items to consider:

Increased Equity

With an increase in space comes an increase in autonomy, although the increase in space usually means an increase in responsibility. Nonetheless, you are in charge of maintaining your space and can control and manipulate it accordingly. So long as you have the capital, you can adjust your living space without having to obtain permission from third parties. This is important as upgrades will affect the value of the home.

Heightened Autonomy

No, not every house exceeds 10,000 square feet – especially not your first house. Yet at the same time, the purchase of a home provides you with more space than "your room" at your parent's place or your dorm room in college. Even if you previously owned an apartment, the benefit of your home is that you do not have to tread lightly for fear of disturbing "neighbors" above and below you.

Real-Road Crossing

Intersection: Possessions + Capital
Purchasing a home is an investment and is usually viewed as the key to financial stability in this country. It also creates an opportunity to build wealth if the investment is nurtured properly.

Business Function

Not only is your home your private sanctuary away from the world, but it is a world unto itself. In addition to functioning as your living space, your home can be utilized as a place of business. For example, many entrepreneurs or small businesses start with home offices.

Further, the house has a recognized value in the real estate market. Both the external and internal visual aesthetics not only reflect the status, tastes and personalities of the people who live inside the home, but also affect the marketability of the home upon resale. Further, where you choose to live will significantly affect your children's educational prospects with respect to public and private schools within your area. Therefore, much consideration should go into the purchase of a home.

HOME IS WHERE THE HOUSE IS

Early in this chapter, you saw that purchasing a car is a process that requires some thought. Likewise, there are several details to consider when evaluating the purchase of "your first home." Since purchasing a home involves more money and more risk than that of a car purchase, it is equally, if not more essential, for you to perform diligent research *before* making this significant purchase. To kick-start your thought process, we highlight just a few – but not *all* – items you should consider before purchasing a home.

First, think of the ideal area that you would like to call home. As discussed previously in *Chapter*

1: Career and *Chapter 2: Education,* location should be a factor in choosing your home. Be aware that it may be easier to start your career in the state where your college is located unless you have a specific plan to help you transition into your intended home state. If you are in the workforce or in graduate school, looking at the real estate market in the area you intend to relocate should represent another factor in your decision-making process. You need to know the standard of living, the vitality of the real estate market as well as the other geographic indicators that may influence your readiness and willingness to purchase a house.

Did you ever hear about the young graduate who was raised in the South, completed their undergraduate education on the West Coast, attended a prestigious graduate school on the East Coast, and is now trying to land a job in the Midwest? Well, do not feel bad if you have not heard of this person, for neither have we. Such "shape-shifting" is not easy to do, especially when you factor that all of the connections and contacts made during undergraduate and professional school are not from the same geographic area. It will be all the more difficult to get your life on track when moving to a totally new state without having established any contacts or mentors beforehand. Therefore, with this in mind, start thinking early about where your want to reside.

Your decision on where to live may also be affected by where and how you obtain certification or licensing for your profession. For example, if you want to become a doctor, not only do you have to complete college, but you must apply to medical school, *then* complete a residency program. Are you looking to receive all of your education and training in the same location? Again, research your plan accordingly.

The decision to purchase a home will also depend upon the type of home desired (e.g., square footage, number of bedrooms, number of bathrooms, basement, storage, & etc.). Essentially, all of the details that amount to *the perfect home* for you.

For example, as a single, gainfully employed Young Adult, you could consider purchasing a townhouse instead of a detached, single-family home, but nonetheless reap similar financial benefits from your investment over the continued rental of an apartment space.

Lastly, you should also research the real estate market in the area you intend to purchase. Do steadily increasing prices indicate that you will likely profit from your investment? How is the crime rate? Has there been a flurry of sales in your prospective neighborhood recently? If so, why? Is the area a desirable one? Are the area schools of quality? Since purchasing a home is such a huge commitment, you want to make sure that your investment is well worth it.

GET YOUR HOUSE IN ORDER

Sure, owning your own home is great. However, you need to consider the impact it will have on every facet of your life. Although a house means more independence, it also means more **responsibility** since there is no leasing office to call and report plumbing, heating or lighting issues whenever there is a problem like you can with an apartment building. In order to address your homeowner issues, you have to thumb through the yellow pages and place the call yourself. Every homeowner has a "story" about their sudden and unexpected induction into the **"joys of homeownership"** club, whereby they had to deal with an unplanned maintenance issue that just flat out comes with the territory. Trust us when we say that you will become quite familiar with your local hardware store.

Maintenance issues will also familiarize you with all of the unique features inside of your home. Be forewarned – maintaining a house of any size will become a continuing financial commitment that you must be prepared to address. Do not be fooled; principal, interest, taxes, and insurance are not your only costs after making a house purchase. *In addition* to your threshold moving costs, prepare to cover the costs of general upkeep and repair, landscaping, painting, appliances, utilities, emergency repair, upgrades, cleaning, furniture, security and the like. Similar to a **car**, do not fudge your budget for a home purchase.

In devising your budget, "standard business practice" should be to set aside capital for (un)expected maintenance. Some months, the most you may have to do is replace a light bulb or a smoke detector battery. Other months, you may have to contend with a broken fence, a flooded basement or an uprooted tree. Prepare for the worst and hope for the best. As a rough rule of thumb, sock away an additional **10%** of your monthly mortgage note for maintenance and repairs. This way, you better manage the impact of unwanted surprises.

KNOW THE FULL PRICE

• down payment	• down payment
• monthly mortgage	• monthly finance charge
- principal	• taxes
- interest	• title
- taxes	• registration fees
- insurance	• replacement of battery
• utilities	• replacement of filters
- gas	• accident insurance
- electric	• gas
- water	• cleaning
- sewage	• oil change
- trash collection	• rotate tires
- phone	• detailing and wax
- cable	• replacement of tires
• natural disasters (e.g.,	• replacement of brake
flood, fallen trees)	pads
• low-level emergencies	• transmission tune-up
(e.g., plumbing)	• emergency road
• landscaping	service
• furniture	• replacement of brake
• interior decoration	light bulbs
• improvements	• replacement of drive
• paint (in and outside)	belt
• general repairs	• repair of minor dents
• fence/border/perimeter	and scratches
• cleaning	• replacement of brake
• security	rotors

When calculating the cost of your happiness, we did not even address what it will take for you to make your space "your own" by investing in a coordinated decorating scheme. Chances are that when you move into your first home, you will also want to purchase new furniture (the plastic crates you used to keep your socks and undies separate may work in your college dorm room but not quite so well in your home).

Recall, this is your **LifeTime** and your success that we are discussing here, so you *must* do that which will make you happy. Just know that if obtaining color-coordinated and fashionable household items is a priority for you, also know how it will impact your budget.

GETTING NEEDS MET

Relationships require maintenance; your "relationship" with your car and/or home is no different. Typically, the more valuable the item, the more it will "cost" you to maintain that relationship.

It is no secret that transportation and housing costs are significant investments. In order to continue extracting value from these items, you must ensure that their needs are MET. At the point of purchase, you should expect an obligation to continually invest your:

M oney

E nergy

T ime

in order to successfully maintain these relationships.

When it comes to major purchases such as a car or a house, there is more to consider than just the list price. Taking this into account, you may actually adjust the type of car or house you purchase so that you are comfortably able to meet all of your obligations, both the stated and the hidden costs. It will not be fun lying awake at night wondering how the mortgage or car note is going to get paid. In retrospect, while we wipe our brow and say sheepishly "Whew! We're glad it worked out," prior planning could have prevented much unnecessary stress.

ASK YOUR FOLKS

What was their first car or home purchase like? How prepared were they for the experience? Would they do anything different?

Sport Utility Vehicle

☑ *Knowing why you really need a car is key.*

Status Utility Vehicle

☑ *Your driving needs vs. what your image wants.*

Wheeling and Dealing

☑ *Know the difference between leasing and financing.*

But, Where to Park?

☑ *Don't just buy a home, invest in one.*

Home Is Where the House Is

☑ *Three rules to live by: location, location, location.*

Get Your House in Order

☑ *Count on the hidden costs of home ownership.*

CONNECT
THE
DOTS

>> *Before you start test driving new cars, test yourself to see if you know retailer terms such as MSRP. The test is you should be able to explain the concept to a younger sibling or cousin in three sentences or less.*

>> *Think of your dream house, then think about its price. How much money will you need to save for a down payment? While you're at it, calculate the monthly payments as well.*

>> *What are the advantages or disadvantages of purchasing a home with a 30-year fixed mortgage versus a 5-year Adjustable Rate Mortgage?*

CHAPTER 5:
COMPANIONSHIP

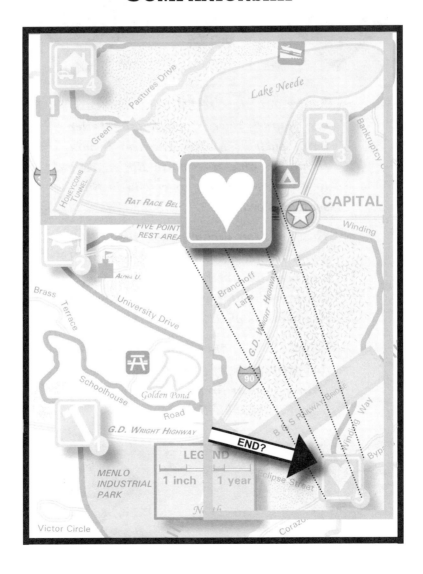

115

THE ROAD AHEAD

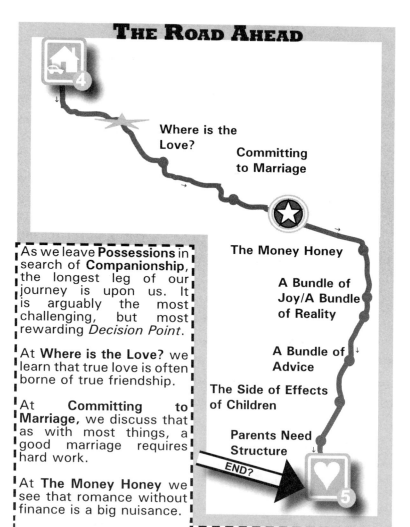

Where is the Love?

Committing to Marriage

The Money Honey

A Bundle of Joy/A Bundle of Reality

A Bundle of Advice

The Side of Effects of Children

Parents Need Structure

END?

As we leave **Possessions** in search of **Companionship**, the longest leg of our journey is upon us. It is arguably the most challenging, but most rewarding *Decision Point*.

At **Where is the Love?** we learn that true love is often borne of true friendship.

At **Committing to Marriage,** we discuss that as with most things, a good marriage requires hard work.

At **The Money Honey** we see that romance without finance is a big nuisance.

At **A Bundle of Joy/A Bundle of Reality/A Bundle of Advice** we learn that having and raising children *the right way* is an exciting, yet humbling responsibility.

Lastly, at **The Side Effects of Children/Parents Need Structure**, we sketch out what parenthood entails.

CHAPTER FIVE
WHO WILL RIDE WITH YOU?

COURSE PREVIEW

For the final stop on our roadmap, we address a most popular destination indeed. This chapter is entitled **Companionship** because it references exploring and discovering relationships with those persons that you genuinely care for and about. More importantly, you want people that you feel positively about to accompany you throughout this journey called life. The nature of this arduous journey is such that positive relationships in your life *can and will* propel you and sustain you for even greater distances.

This is why we focus on core-family connections since by design, they are more permanent in nature and are longer lasting. We take a few moments here to address these familial connections in two primary categories – *spouse* and *children* – since they can (and do) drastically affect the direction of even the most thoroughly-planned roadmap. But perhaps more importantly, what is the point of successfully navigating the other four *Decision Points* if you have no one to share your hard-fought **success** with?

That being said, we understand that marriage or having children may not be one of your overall goals. However, feel free to apply some of the practical pointers in the section about marriage to other relationships in your life. As for the advice pertaining to children, pass it along to a friend if you are not interested quite yet.

WHERE IS THE LOVE?

For those of you who ardently desire to meet your star-crossed companion one day, here is a well kept secret: you probably have the best chance of finding a spouse while in college for two reasons: 1) frequency of contact with potential candidates and 2) an available pool of candidates.

Do not take the above two statements as advice that you should go to college just so you can find a spouse, but realize that by being immersed in that environment, you improve your chances of finding a lifelong soulmate. Once you start working and have a fixed schedule (i.e., the "daily grind"), it may become more difficult to meet people outside of your regular routine and workplace.

Once you settle into the regular routine of work, professional school or managing your own business, it is all the more difficult to randomly "bump into" your dream date (e.g., while at the grocery store or while doing laundry). Oh, and good luck finding someone at a bar or a club – it is not as easy as they make it seem like in the movies or on TV!

RUSHING TOWARDS ETERNITY

Now if and when you finally find Mr. or Mrs. Right, you will be faced with plenty of heart-wrenching decisions. The first of which is the over-arching question of **LOVE**. If you are truly in love, then what exactly is the rush to get married if you intend to share all of eternity together? Think about it. No one wakes up and says to themselves, "You know, I want to get married three different times in this **LifeTime**." The idea is to do it once and to do it right. And for those individuals who despite their parents' divorce, adjusted to life just fine, it is safe to assume that they too, do not wake up daily and say to themselves, "You know, I want to raise my kids to live in a divorced household."

The statistics are staggering. Roughly half of all marriages end in divorce, with most divorces occurring within the first five years! With this being the case, make the proper investment at the beginning of the relationship so that you are in a better position to ensure that your union lasts a **LifeTime**. We cannot tell you from personal experience, but from what we have learned watching friends and associates, getting a divorce is not as easy as hanging up a phone on an obtuse boyfriend or girlfriend.

As arcane as it sounds, we recommend a *full courtship* before marriage so that you have the opportunity to experience your future partner over an extended period of time among different scenarios and settings. Once married, you just cannot leave the restaurant after an argument, go home, cool off and later make an apologetic phone call. When you cross the threshold of marriage, first, one of you has to pay the bill – ostensibly with funds that you both share. Then, you both have to drive home together from the restaurant and sleep under the same roof, and (presumably) the same bed. A long courtship provides the framework for establishing a life-long friendship that can better withstand such tiffs that may occur.

Also, remember that by the time you meet your special someone, they have been living without you and your long-term relationship for quite some time. Therefore, some of their quirks, pet peeves and bad habits may come as a surprise to you during the beginning of the marriage. After your first year of marriage, you may think that you have been misled due to how much your spouse "has changed," but the reality may be that you are now being exposed to the more intimate layers of your friendship.

Cheesy but True:

It is not easy finding the perfect person who is willing to accept all of your imperfections.

Do not get discouraged about the idiosyncrasies that you discover about your spouse: generally speaking, your spouse does not drastically change after marriage, but rather *your perspective* of them does. Often, many people set extremely high standards for the person that they are looking to spend the rest of their life with – essentially they require that their potential spouse be perfect. As a result, many people formulate good, strong relationships only to abandon them under the belief that there is still "someone or something better out there."

Watch for Bull:

I love my spouse but cannot stand her parents! Before you fall into this "anti-in-law" trap, answer this quick question: who provided your spouse with her current DNA? Since they are all related, it is best to learn as much as you can about everybody.

While it is commendable to desire and seek out certain qualities in a particular spouse, the danger comes in limiting yourself to this ideal list. Some flexibility has to occur. As with any relationship, there will have to be some give and take, so you might as well prepare for this fact now. This is not to discourage you from seeking out your vision of your destined mate, but to caution you from being too rigid in your search.

Cheesy but True:

There are always other fish in the sea. True, but take care to mind the waters in which you tread: beware of the swelling riptide, stinging jellyfish, circling sharks, and the calls of those already lost at sea.

THAT MAGICAL DAY

Sharon: *I am happily married to my best friend. It* **was** *the laughter, fun, culture, and adventure that first attracted us to one another while in a foreign land. Now, it* **is** *the commitment to one another, loyalty to our relationship and union of our hearts that will keep us ever committed to maintaining an eternity of happiness. You see, my husband and I met while studying abroad and maintained a friendship for over a three-year period that my husband says began when I started looking at him "funny" one day a few months after we met (now you know it was* **he** *who started looking at me funny* **first***).*

In any event, the friendship blossomed into a relationship more splendid that any romance novel. Even though I "officially" vowed to commit my heart, body and mind to a union with my destined mate on our wedding day, this ritual only confirmed what had already transpired between us. In essence, our friendship had previously laid the foundation for the love that grew and ignited a passion to commit the rest of our lives together. To this day, we maintain our friendship and romance with the same amount of passion, because we take time to nurture and grow it as with any relationship.

Frederick: *The day I married my wife, it was a magical day indeed. But when I say magical, let me tell you what* **did not** *happen. What did not happen was that every other woman on the planet through some simultaneous, seismic, electrical purple shock turned ugly and deformed. No.* **That did not occur.** *So that means that to this day, otherwise attractive ladies roam the planet (again, I cannot confirm this, but merely submit this statement with all due humility and respect based upon what I vaguely recall being told some time ago when I was half-paying attention).*

But guess what? Our wedding day was "magical" in that I made a decision that I would see "The Queen" as the most beautiful lady on the planet. Period. I also put to rest the illusion that I would find something "better," because for me, there is no such thing. My friends, believe me when I say that what I have is plenty magical . . .

COMMITTING TO MARRIAGE

In addition to committing to your spouse, *you need to make a commitment to the marriage itself.* For now, as a married couple, you are a legal entity, much like a **partnership**. Hence, your family is composed of three parts: you, your spouse and the marriage.

The institution of marriage is probably the most emotionally, spiritually and financially rewarding institution that there is (we do not consider kids to be an "institution" although they can possibly send you to one). In managing your partnership, the goal is for you and your spouse to amass a wealth of loving memories to share in perpetuity. Since true wealth can endure for generations, it behooves you to choose your mate carefully.

Cheesy but True:

A lover of the heart easily flutters away, while a friend at heart beats to your rhythm all day.

When seeking your eternal companion, marry a good mind, not just a good body or income. If you marry one of the latter, you will soon discover that the relationship often leaves once the body or income starts to fail. Too many marriages fail because of inflated expectations (and body parts!). Of course, there are moments in which you can/will/should feel that your marriage is a non-stop magical ride to the land of physical bliss and ecstasy. But let's face it. It will not feel that way at all times, and this is where true friendship becomes very important, for true friendships have the unique ability to improve and grow over time. It is easier to weather the journey of life with a tried and true friend rather than with a tired and false acquaintance.

Now to be clear, there is nothing wrong with being physically attracted to the person you want to spend the rest of your life with. In fact, we recommend it – such attraction makes for cuter babies. But seriously, equally as important as the exterior makeup of your spouse is the interior. How beautiful or handsome are they on the inside? Realize that at some point in the future, their external look will undergo some change (as will yours). It is inevitable. The rules of time say so. Thus, you want to have a companion that you get along with when gravity takes over (ask your folks what we mean).

THE MONEY HONEY

Do you remember your first movie date? The finances were exceedingly simple then. Either you engaged in the American tradition of "going Dutch," (i.e., shared the cost of the tickets), or one of you decided to treat the other. Important topics dominated the discussion such as what either had seen on TV the night before or the upcoming school dance. Now, back to the future. In today's day and age, money and finances are a significant part of most marriages.

Although you may love and respect your marriage partner deeply, you need to be honest that finances can potentially become a very touchy subject, regardless of the amount at stake. Since this will more than likely be the first time that you share a bank account or finances with anyone, you should prepare yourself for an adjustment period. Your marriage will undoubtedly suffer if the two of you are simply unable to sustain yourselves financially. So, make sure that you take time and communicate directly your ideas about finances often and early with your spouse.

Married couples comprise two individuals who had separate bank accounts before their union. Upon marrying, many couples open a joint bank account. However, their thinking may still be based on an individualistic mentality, meaning, each spouse has not fully adopted a couple-first philosophy. In order to do so, a couple needs to evaluate and address how each other values money so that there is a clear understanding of the family budget.

Granted, different couples do different things. But let's focus on that ambiguous majority: If you are a couple who has decided to "share your love, time and worldly possessions" with one another then "your" money becomes "our" money. Even with separate accounts, the subject of finances will directly affect your relationship in tangible ways. Couples are given basic directives before they marry: work hard and save as much as you can; make sure to invest in the stock market, etc. However, not that many couples are counseled directly about aligning their resources into a shared system for the couple. Most people thinking individually, believe that their way is the best way to manage money. Or, some people just assume that their way is the *only* way and do not consider any other perspectives. Either may apply in your situation, but in all practical terms you want to avoid conflict by creating a communication and money-minded system that you both agree to respect – *ahead of time.*

By addressing this important issue early on in your union, you can avoid major fallouts over seemingly minor confrontations. For example, why it is OK for you to get this monthly magazine subscription, but it is not OK for your spouse to get their caramel frappuccino every morning? These seemingly small issues can compound over time and become truly bothersome over time. Then, you run the additional risk of having these latent issues unnecessarily exacerbate future seemingly "unrelated" confrontations.

Real-Road Crossing

Intersection: Capital + Companionship
Although the best things in life are for free, prepare for the costs of married life and family life (e.g., day care, private school, family vacations, etc.).

There will also be a need for compromise between both spouses on the items that each individual needs or wants. In fact, there will be lots of late-night conversations about some of the following: *Can we afford a new home? A new car? How about a weekend getaway? Or a new microwave for goodness sakes? What nice thing can we do for our anniversary? Can we afford to have another baby?* Whether it is the big screen TV or the custom-made drapes that match the couches, there will be a compromise of needs and wants.

Needless to say, talking frequently about the finances can do wonders for a couple. First, the more that you discuss them, the less tense and anxious the conversation should be. Secondly, such exchanges provide an opportunity for you both to continually evaluate your spending habits and savings techniques. The object is to avoid money becoming a source of tension, arguments, disagreements and headaches – for there is plenty else to discuss in running a household – especially one that comes with children.

A BUNDLE OF JOY

Kids are great!

A BUNDLE OF REALITY

Kids are a great challenge!

A BUNDLE OF ADVICE

Another major factor that impacts Young Adult life is the introduction of new life: **CHILDREN!** Since having a child is a life-changing experience, it is generally a good idea to know ahead of time when you want your life changed. In short, we recommend planning for children. A little planning will help ensure that you have certain aspects of your life in place so that you can fully enjoy the presence of this new person in your life. Things to think about include: *How will a new child affect the development of your career? Or better yet, your education? Who will be the child's primary caregivers? What about the costs of raising a child? Yes! Costs!*

Many Young Adults contemplating children do not think of this topic in capitalistic terms – perhaps this is in response to an almost instinctual repulsion to think of kids in such an analytical manner. As we discussed in *Chapter 3: Capital,* you need money to survive and this principle equally applies to your children as you must provide basic necessities for your children: food, clothing, shelter, schooling, etc. But funny thing is, although kids "need money," all they really want is time – your time in particular. Since **time is money**, invest time now planning how you will spend your money, energy and time with those who stand to carry forth your legacy.

Real-Road Crossing

__Intersection: Capital + Companionship__
When planning for children, also plan for activities/toys/school/ childcare, all of which require investments of time and money.

With respect to making time for your future progeny, there is a school of thought which suggests that having kids should be natural (i.e., unplanned). Hey, if you really want to be natural, then you should also give up microwaves, dishwashers and electricity. At the same time, we are not necessarily advocating that people go so far as to try to "time" things so that their potential child will have a particular birthday.

This being said, there is probably never a "perfect" time to have kids. But at least you can be prepared for that time if and when it comes. There are two major schools of though regarding child-bearing. One approach is to have kids while you are still relatively young (e.g., early 20s). In this instance, you can use your youth as a buffer to help raise them and relate to them and grow a close relationship. The con to this is that you may struggle financially because you may not have built up the financial strength that raising a child requires. Yet, it goes without saying that it is easier to have children *after finishing school* as opposed to finishing school *after having children*.

It's LifeTime!

The second approach is to make some money early on, gain more financial security, get your career established somewhat, then have kids later in life (e.g., mid-30s). The con to this is a larger generation gap, and possible lack of patience and youth to handle child-rearing effectively.

We are not saying that it cannot be done – that you cannot reverse the order and find a spouse, have kids early and then start upon your road to riches. Just realize the pros and cons of each decision. On one hand, it may be "easier" to find someone with similar interests while in college, but having kids early may require extra energy to put in the work necessary to still make your big breakthrough. However, if you have kids early (whether intentionally or not) just realize the potential effects this may have on your earning capability. Ironically, once the kids come around and you finally discover how much of your resources raising them will require, you may need to revisit your **Career** goals.

After all, to truly enjoy this **LifeTime**, remain mindful of the cost you need to pay in exchange for your desired *success*. Everything has its cost and price. When it comes to the price of your time and energy on the open market, you will only command the best price if you are "the best" in what you do. In order to be the best, you must prepare to sacrifice plenty of hours studying and training with no guarantee of success. While in school or during your first few years in the field, there may not be a whole lot of time left for family or close friends while you throw yourself to your work, gain experience in your craft and educate yourself about the rules of the road.

For instance, if you obtain a $100K+ salaried position, whether in the public or private sector, expect that a regular work week will extend well beyond the traditional forty-hour work week schedule. With increased salary comes increased responsibility. Further, in high-salary positions, many people feel a nagging obligation to "finish the job" before leaving home for the night, rather than to be the first one in the parking lot at 5:01 PM. Start thinking now about how you will balance the tension between making money for your family versus making time for your family.

Very rare is the individual who obtains financial success by barely lifting a finger. More likely, you will have to spend time, time, and even more time on your task. You may have to "stay late" when everyone else has gone home, or get up extra early, or sacrifice your weekends, or make an appearance at social functions that are of no interest to you. Whatever the case – these are all activities that will require your time.

Be mindful about how these expenditures will affect your personal life, especially if you plan to have a spouse or children. How will your absence affect them? Is it best to wait until you achieve a certain level of success before developing these relationships? But what if that level never comes? Remember, money does not grow on trees – it grows in seeds that you plant firmly in the sod of sacrifice and fertilize with the sweat of your brow.

The other reality is that your earning potential may suffer due to the responsibilities of parenthood (i.e., more time with kids = less time making money). So, you will have to plan for the type of impact that being a parent may have on your overall roadmap as well as the other *Decision Points* that await you: **Career, Education, Capital** and **Possessions**.

No Magic Here:

Key Considerations for Child-Rearing
→ *Impact on Career path*
→ *Additional expenses*
→ *Childcare options*
→ *Your geographic location*

THE SIDE EFFECTS OF CHILDREN

Are you a patient person? If not, you will soon become one. This is just one of the many benefits that you will acquire by virtue of your new role as a parent. Check out some additional possible "side effects" of having kids:

>> *eating cold food*
>> *possible weight gain*
>> *bleary eyes (from sleep deprivation)*
>> *facial wrinkles (from furrowed brow)*
>> *stain-filled clothes*
>> *hair loss (from pulling)*
>> *loss of adult television programming*
>> *growth of two left feet*
>> *loss of spontaneity*
>> *loss of adult vocabulary*

>> NOTE <<

Any "loss" of hearing sustained by male fathers is considered suspect. Informal studies show that male fathers hear quite clearly the infant child screaming during odd hours of the night despite a sudden increase in snoring that suggests the contrary.

For the most part, we are joking here. But the practical reality is that your life will change. Your social life will not be the same. You simply will have to spend your time in different ways. Bottom line: do not be afraid to discuss child rearing early and often – for your lives will be forever changed.

What exactly do we mean? Well, in addition to the large, obvious changes that your life will undergo, there are also scores of more minor, but significant changes that will constantly confront you. For instance, even though you purchased dinner for your hungry children with your hard-earned money, they may not eat it because they changed their mind without warning. But guess what? You *still* need to feed them later, irrespective of what your checking account thinks. In addition, your entire pace of life changes. No longer will you zip around town when handling your errands. Going to the grocery store now becomes an event. "Popping in" the post office for more stamps can now become a major chore.

Thanks to federal regulations, you have to have your child in some sort of car seat apparatus until approximately the age of eight and sixty pounds. This means that it will take you additional time to get in and out of the car. You will now wrestle with vexing decisions such as: *Am I going to be out long enough to have to bring out the stroller?* And, please recall, kids are free spirits. They use the bathroom when they please, get hungry whenever, and fall asleep when tired. Period. Sometimes, kids being kids may interfere severely with your pre-conceived adult plans.

Sure, love always finds a way and you cannot plan everything – but to the extent that you are able, you can try to execute a plan. After all, **luck is the residue of design**. We caution against the attitude of "we'll just work it out" serving as your *only* safeguard. However noble and positive that it is, it is still vague. Why struggle unnecessarily if you do not have to?

No Magic Here:

Kids are little people with deceptively large personalities! Plan and prepare to have both the time and patience to effectively shape their experiences to reflect and reinforce the values that your family shares.

PARENTS NEED STRUCTURE

We are well aware and fully realize that often in the movies or on TV, that we frequently see the classic suburban soccer mom handling every detail of family life with ease, efficiency and minimal effort. Great. Let's just assume that you will not have the benefit of trick photography to make you look as good. On the following page is a "sample" day in your future life. *The Scenario:* you are (happily) married, and (happily) have two kids under five years old. *NOTE: actual results will vary.*

⤵ 5:58 AM

>> The kids wake up.

⤵ 6:10 AM

>> You wake up.

>> You nudge your spouse and greet the toddler while you change the infant's diaper.

>> You jump in the shower.

>> You jump out the shower and hurriedly dress yourself.

>> You pick out the toddler's clothes and direct your spouse to change the toddler.

>> You make up your bed, make up the infant's bed and "help" the toddler make up his bed.

>> You make breakfast for the family – really the kids.

>> You make new formula bottles for the infant while washing the old ones.

>> You make lunch for the toddler.

>> You pack lunch for yourself.

>> You empty the dishwasher.

>> You feed the baby, you brush everybody's teeth (including your spouse's).

>> You make pointless protests about "not wanting to be late."

>> You load everyone into the car.

>> You drop off the kids at day care and preschool (in two different locations).

>> You work a full day (and deal with whatever "drama" that happens at work).
>> You pick up the kids from day care and preschool.
>> You retrieve the mail (read: bills).
>> You change out of your work clothes/ uniform.
>> You take the toddler to dance-enrichment lessons.
>> You cook dinner.
>> You wait for your spouse's return and dash out to the gym to go "workout."
>> You return to wipe down the stove, clean the kitchen table and sweep the kitchen floor.
>> You start baths for the kids.
>> You put the kids in their pajamas.
>> You read the kids a book apiece.
>> You put the kids to bed.

➲ **8:37 PM**
>> After putting your kid to bed, you flop down in the nearest chair and wonder where the day went!

Now, you have time to get up from the chair and pay bills, do laundry, clean the rest of the house and prepare for your next day at work. Hey! You might even want to squeeze in some time to read for leisure, take some personal phone calls or God forbid, watch some cable television. If it sounds like a lot, why, it *IS* a lot. Once kids are present and accounted for, your day will likely revolve around their schedule (i.e., their wants and needs, not yours).

Sharon: *If you are enjoying the vigors of child rearing while trying to mount a career, then you definitely have your work cut out for you – both inside and outside of the home.*

Frederick: *I shall never forget learning how to handle this awesome responsibility of "family" with my first-born son. The obvious had never occurred to me, but I remember exclaiming towards the end of his first week home: "You mean, we have to bathe him every night!?!?" Please. Try not to laugh (too loudly). It was an honest oversight on my part. All my life, I only had to worry about cleaning up after myself. Even when married, what the Queen did on her time was her business. Now, I had to think about someone else the same way I did myself. This my friends, is sometimes easier said than done!*

You should also consider that doing all of the "little" things to become financially successful will affect your schedule with the wee ones. For instance, working a full day, then networking at night, taking work home, and working on weekends all add up to time away from the kids. Ideally, working an eight-hour day would be enough to advance your career, and provide for your growing family. Yet, this is less and less the case; the market does not pay like this. Just be mindful and plan accordingly – *ahead of time.*

When seeking companionship in the form of spouse and children, take time to reflect on how these personal relationships in your life will affect your roadmap and vice versa. Finding a spouse is no easy task in your day and age. Similarly, raising a child is an awesome responsibility that has a variety of implications for your life. Therefore, careful consideration must be given to both decisions since who you share your **LifeTime** with is arguably one of the most important questions that you will ever have to definitively answer. There is no time like the present to get started on your balancing act . . .

No Magic Here:

Having kids is not a hobby, but rather a full-time commitment. There are no days off, but plenty of overtime.

ASK YOUR FOLKS

Determine what was more important to your folks when they were your age – starting a family early or getting a jump-start on their career?

REARVIEW REVIEW

Where is the Love?

☑ *True love is often borne of true friendship.*

Committing to Marriage

☑ *Like most things, marriage requires work.*

The Money Honey

☑ *Romance without finance is a big nuisance.*

A Bundle of Joy/A Bundle of Reality

☑ *Kids are precious – well, most of the time.*

A Bundle of Advice

☑ *Prepare if you dare to have kids.*

The Side Effects of Children

☑ *Patience is not just a virtue, it is virtually guaranteed.*

Parents Need Structure

☑ *Your world revolves around your kids, not you!*

CONNECT
THE
DOTS

>> *Make a list of three successful people that you admire. Make two columns: spouse and children and determine the marital status of these individuals and whether they have children.*

>> *For your three individuals, do you see any patterns? Which came first, the companionship or the success?*

>> *Plan on getting married? Try this exercise: go to the grocery store with your potential new spouse and a sample fixed budget (e.g., $150) to buy groceries for one week. See what you both agree upon and what you think are "frivolous" choices by the other.*

CONCLUSION: IT'S LIFETIME!

WHO are you? WHO do you want to be?
WHO do you want to meet? WHO will you
work with? WHO will you love? WHO will
respect you? WHO will pay you for your
time? WHAT do you want to do? WHAT will
it cost you? **WHAT** must you sacrifice?
WHAT can you do? WHAT is it worth?
WHAT will keep you stimulated? WHAT
will keep you satisfied? WHEN will you
get started? WHEN do you think you will
be ready? WHEN will you know that
you made it? WHEN will you **WHEN**
will you start? WHERE do you want to
be? **WHERE** can you get started? WHERE
can you find reliable help? WHERE do
you want to live? **WHY** succeed? WHY
try? WHY chase after your dreams? WHY
believe? WHY is it worth it? WHY do you
want what you think you want? WHY
are you unsure? WHY do you think
you know the answer? **HOW** will you
succeed? HOW will you execute your
plan? HOW did you get started? HOW
exactly will you know when it is time to

CONCLUSION
TIME IS OF THE ESSENCE

Now that our time with you is drawing to a close, we will briefly review the ground we have covered so far.

As mentioned earlier, whether you travel along the *Rat Race* track or take the long, winding *Road to Success*, you will likely encounter one or all the five major **Decision Points**. Your definition of success will guide you in developing a practical roadmap to your destination. So far, we have highlighted several practical pointers to consider along your journey and will now revisit some of those ideas. To start with, let's review our working roadmap and *Decision Points*.

ROADMAP to SUCCESS

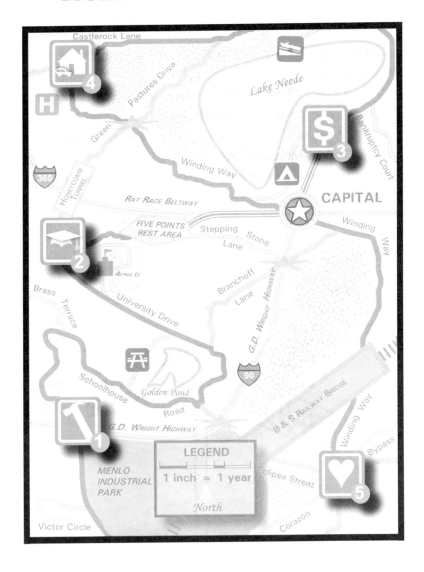

CAREER

to have a successful, fulfilling and rewarding occupation

EDUCATION

to gain the respect and admiration of peers and the public for being genuinely qualified and skilled at your craft

CAPITAL

to obtain sufficient cash and credit to comfortably finance your desired lifestyle

POSSESSIONS

to apply your capital towards the acquisition of objects (e.g., car, house) that tangibly represent your success

COMPANIONSHIP

to blissfully share your lifestyle with your dream mate and/or to have smart, healthy and beautiful children that further your legacy

YOU HAVE SOME TIME,
BUT NOT A LOT OF TIME

Consider the following analogy; think of your life as a mixture of wet cement. If you have ever seen a cement truck, they are rather unique because they contain these conical-shaped drums that keep rotating – even when the vehicle is not in motion. Why does the cylinder keep spinning? So that the cement mixture inside maintains its moisture and does not sit still and harden. Once the cement is laid down on the ground, say in the shape of a sidewalk square, and is exposed to air, the clock starts ticking. The more that time passes, it becomes more difficult to change or mold the shape of the cement. With the passage of time, the cement begins to dry and becomes more hard and less malleable in the process.

Your life is very similar to the cement mixture in the back of the truck. Once you enter the world of "adulthood" (i.e., decide about your career, obtain an education, etc.) you will find it exceedingly difficult to move or shift from your current position. In other words, think of your grandparents' lives as the equivalent of dry cement and the lives of your parents as being in the *final* phases of hardening. Finally, as a Young Adult, you are in the *early* phases of hardening – so, you have more opportunities to mold the shape that your cement takes.

Your folks, we are sure, are all wonderfully dynamic people, but believe us when we say that they simply do not have the same flexibility of choice and options that you currently have. Actually, do not take our word for it, just ask your folks! We are sure that they will help you realize the advantage you hold since your "cement is relatively fresh," and may be molded in almost anyway that you desire. Finally, we firmly believe that *thinking concretely about your situation helps make your situation more concrete*. It therefore behooves you to take full advantage of your flexibility now and plan ahead! So remember, the more planning and research that goes into your decision-making, the more likely you are to succeed in this **LifeTime**.

DID WE MENTION THE WORD "PLAN"?

Very few things are created out of thin air. Most things are created by design, meaning, someone first had to come up with a plan. Not coincidentally, the greater the task, the greater the planning. Just curious, but how many people do you know just "spontaneously" build aircraft carriers? We personally do not know that many given the extensive planning that such a massive project requires. In this respect, consider yourself the chief architect charged with the task of building a hugely successful life. To truly become successful, *make plans to be successful.*

No Bones about It:

Often times, it takes twenty years of planning and preparation to make an overnight success.

It goes without saying that a concrete plan *is not absolutely necessary* since you might also attain your desired lifestyle by chance, circumstance or just plain ol' good fortune. Conversely, even with a plan in place, you may not fulfill your goals for a myriad of reasons. Therefore, we cannot guarantee that mere possession of a roadmap or plan for your life will automatically transform your life into a successful one. However, **we can guarantee** that *without a plan* in place, reaching your goals successfully will become all the more difficult.

The reason why planning during this "Young Adult" phase of your life is so important is because you possess tremendous flexibility to choose among a wide range of options that will undoubtedly shape the course of your entire life (e.g., the "cement is relatively fresh"). If you are looking for a cost-efficient tool to help keep you focused, this is where a plan or **roadmap** will come in handy.

When we encourage Young Adults to "plan now to profit later," we view the roadmap-making process as useful in creating tangible expectations for success. Further, the very process of creating a plan encourages honesty about what you already know and *what you need to learn more about*. Make no mistake about it – even with a plan in place, you will *still* inevitably make mistakes. Further, without proper planning and preparation, you leave yourself even *more* vulnerable to *manageable* and *preventable* mistakes that may negatively impact your overall chances for success.

While it is not necessary (or possible) to have all of your life "mapped out" in excruciating detail, do yourself a favor and at least make out a rough sketch. This way, *you can at least have an idea about the general direction in which you wish to travel*. You can always change your mind in the future – but first make it up! Many Young Adults do not take full advantage of the early opportunity to reflect on their *Road to Success* and consequently end up spinning their wheels within the *Rat Race* instead. We believe that if you plan ahead, you will enable yourself to think your way out of this predicament – *ahead of time.*

C'mon now, be honest. Who sets out in life to fail? Who plans to be ignorant? Who plans to be broke? Who plans to be homeless? Who plans for heartbreak? Who plans for despair? The idea is that your life is the substance of dreams; dreams that need money, energy and time to convert them into realities. There is simply no time like the present to build up your life-chances, with planning and preparation as your tools.

PARTING THOUGHTS

Okay! Are you ready for **Life**? Well, not quite. We just have a few more things to tell you. More specifically, if you have not guessed already, we heavily advocate that you develop a plan for your life's success and happiness. In other words, if you can envision what will make you happy, then you can develop a plan towards realizing it. Why? It is our belief that with a plan in place, not only do you increase your likelihood of completing your desired goals, but you also improve your ability to recognize unplanned, yet enriching opportunities when they cross your path.

Even though this book focuses on five major *Decision Points* (e.g., **Career, Education, Capital, Possessions** and *Companionship*), it is understood that each topic may not be applicable to you depending upon your own personal goals. It is also understood that there may be additional aspects about life you deem essential to your journey that are not mentioned here. No problemo – to thine own self stay true.

Before you go, however, what follows are some basic **Road Rules** we wish to share with you:

 ROAD RULES

1) **Keep focused on the road ahead.** *Aside from brief glances, you may not spend a long time gazing into the rearview mirror.*

2) **Plan on changing your plan.** *You must always keep your eyes open for alternate routes since there are NO guarantees on the open road – even with a roadmap in hand.*

3) **Start your journey with your destination in mind.** *You have a long way to go if you do not know where you are going.*

4) **Enjoy the ride.** *Recall, "this thing called life" is a journey, not a singular destination; plan to enjoy the process as much as possible.*

OK! Enough theory, time to practice. We now conclude so that you may begin. Wait a minute . . . do you hear that? *The clock is ticking!* The **Time of Your Life** awaits you!

Ready?

Get set . . .

Now GO!